ONCE UPON A TIME
IN
RUSSIA

ONCE UPON A TIME
IN
RUSSIA

The Rise of the Oligarchs and the Greatest Wealth in History

BEN
MEZRICH

125 YEARS

WILLIAM HEINEMANN: LONDON

1 3 5 7 9 10 8 6 4 2

William Heinemann
20 Vauxhall Bridge Road
London SW1V 2SA

William Heinemann is part of the Penguin Random House group of companies
whose addresses can be found at global.penguinrandomhouse.com.

The names of many of the characters and locations in this book have been changed,
as have many physical characteristics and other descriptive details. Some of the events
and characters are also composites of several different events and persons.

Copyright © Ben Mezrich 2015

Ben Mezrich has asserted his right to be identified as the author of this
Work in accordance with the Copyright, Designs and Patents Act 1988.

First published by William Heinemann in 2015
(First published in the United States by Atria Books, an imprint of Simon & Schuster Inc. in 2015)

www.randomhouse.co.uk

A CIP catalogue record for this book is available from the British Library.

ISBN 9780434023400 (Hardback)
ISBN 9780434023417 (Trade Paperback)

Interior design by Dana Sloan.

Printed and bound in Great Britain by Clays Ltd, St Ives Plc

MIX
Paper from
responsible sources
FSC® C018179

Penguin Random House is committed to a sustainable future for our business,
our readers and our planet. This book is made from Forest Stewardship
Council® certified paper.

AUTHOR'S NOTE

*O*NCE UPON A TIME IN RUSSIA is a dramatic narrative account based on numerous interviews, multiple first-person sources—most of whom have asked to remain anonymous—and thousands of pages of court documents. In some instances, settings have been changed, and certain descriptions have been altered to protect privacy. I employ the technique of re-created dialogue, based on the recollection of participants who were there, court documents, and newspaper accounts, doing my best to communicate the substance of these conversations, especially in scenes taking place more than a decade ago.

PART ONE

A good man, maybe. But it's best to shoot him.

—OLD RUSSIAN PROVERB

CHAPTER ONE

July 2000,
Kuntsevo Dacha, Fili District

THE SILENCE WAS EXCRUCIATING, the minutes ticking by thick and heavy, time itself gorging on the tension in the humid air. Even though the shades had been drawn back from the trio of windows pocking the long plaster walls of the cavernous dining room, it was impossible to tell how deep into the afternoon the day had drifted; the dense forest that surrounded the isolated, two-story compound cast deep shadows across the reinforced glass panes, shifting whatever remained of the bright summer light toward an ominous, gunmetal gray.

For the eighteen middle-aged men in dark suits shifting uncomfortably in their seats as they waited in that palpable silence around an oversize dining room table, it was hard to believe that they were still technically within Moscow's city limits. Though, to be fair, this aging, stone house tucked in the middle of the dark woods, surrounded by a pair of chain-link fences topped by barbed wire, was a symbol of a much different Moscow than the rapidly growing metropolis beyond the wire. The men in this room had traveled back in time more than fifty years the minute they had been ushered out of their chauffeured limousines—now parked in glistening rows behind the double fences—and led through the dacha's front door.

The setting of the meeting was not lost on any of the men. The invitation that had been delivered by official courier to each of them in the preceding weeks had been met by everything from incredulous laughter to expressions of suspicion. Every soul knew what this place was: whose house this had once been, and what had supposedly taken place here. None of the men looked carefully into the shadows that played across the aging walls, darkening the corners of the vast, high-ceilinged room.

Even though this house had fallen into disuse a generation ago—and was now more museum than functioning dacha—the meeting's address had meaning far beyond the invitation itself. And the longer the men were forced to wait for whatever was going to happen next, the more ominous the setting seemed.

Under the best of circumstances, these men were not accustomed to waiting. To describe them as powerful businessmen—or even billionaires—would have been a laughable understatement. Among them, they represented the largest—and fastest—accumulation of wealth in modern history. Within the Russian media, they had garnered the label *Oligarchs*—a term that was usually derogatory, defining them as a class apart and above. According to the popular notion, over the course of the past decade, as the former Soviet nation had lurched into capitalism through a complex, often shadowy process of privatization, this class—the Oligarchs—had accumulated insane riches, and they had used this wealth to imbed and twist themselves, like strangling vines, into the ruling mechanisms of the nation's government, economy, and culture.

Most of the men in this room would have bristled at the designation. If anything, they saw themselves as representatives of the new, free, and modern Russia. Almost all of them had come from poverty; many had clawed their way out of childhoods filled with deprivation and prejudice. Many at one point had been mathematicians, scientists, or academics before they had turned their ambitions to business. If they had succeeded—and yes, as a group they had succeeded to a degree perhaps unique in history—it was *despite* the chronic corruption and cronyism of the shifting Russian paradigm, not because of it.

Oligarchs or not, men who earned billions were not known for their patience. Eventually, the silence got the better of the room, and one of the invitees, seated closest to the door that led back into the interior of the house, cleared his throat.

"If some Chechen managed to get a bomb in here and blew us all to hell," he asked, "do you think anyone would mourn?"

Awkward laughter riffed through the room, then trickled away into the shadows. The macabre joke may have hit too close to home. Whatever the men thought about themselves, it wasn't exactly the best time to be a billionaire in Russia. Worse yet, the idea of a bomb going off in the dining room of such an ominous address wasn't as far-fetched as they would have liked to believe.

Before anyone could break the silence again, there was a rush of motion—a door opening on the far side of the dining room. The air seemed to tighten still further, like a leather strap suddenly pulled taut. After a brief pause, a lone man entered through the doorway. Head down, every step and movement controlled and determined, from his forceful, athletic gait to the way his lean, muscled arms shifted stiffly at his sides. Short of stature—five foot seven at the most—with thinning hair, pinpoint eyes, a narrow, almost daggered jaw—his presence was somehow well beyond the amalgamation of his parts. As he strolled in, warmly shaking each man's hand in turn, none of the billionaires at the table could have turned away even if they had dared. He didn't just project an imposing aura: he was a mystery, an unknown, and these gathered businessmen had built their lives—and fortunes—on their abilities to procure and use knowledge. Even though some of them had been responsible for their host's ascension to power—had in fact hand-picked him for the role he now played—they had done so without knowing much about him. In truth, that had been one of his main selling points. He was purposefully obscure, a supposed nobody—a loyal cog. They had thought that a man like that would be easy to control.

There was nothing easy about him as he took position at the front of the room, facing the table.

And then he smiled.

"*Добро пожаловать.*"

A warm welcome, my colleagues.

He looked around the room, matching each of the gathered billionaire's eyes.

"Some of you supported me," he continued, his voice low and steady, as he paused on a few of the staring faces.

"Some of you did not."

Again, he lingered on a handful more.

"But none of that matters now. You have done very well for yourselves. You have built vast fortunes."

He waited, the room as silent and still as a pane of glass.

"You can keep what you have. Business is important. Industry is important. But from here on out, you are simply businessmen—and *only* businessmen."

Before any of the men could react, there was another flash of motion—and then a group of lower-ranking officials took over, ushering a team of butlers into the room, each carrying a tray laden with porcelain and gold tea settings. Collective relief moved around the table; at the same time, it dawned on most of the men in the room that they had made an immense miscalculation. This loyal nobody, this obscure cog had become something else. Every moment of the meeting had been choreographed, from the very moment he had invited them here, to this place, imbued with so much brutal meaning.

Just a few yards down, off the hall now bustling with servers carrying tea into the dining room, were the study and living quarters where Joseph Stalin had spent his final two decades. This house—Stalin's Moscow home—had been the symbolic headquarters of the most infamous, powerful, and brutal regime in their nation's history.

And Vladimir Putin—the man at the front of the room now trading niceties with the nearest of his guests, while butlers served tea up and down the dining room table—had just sent them a clear, explicit message.

Putin was not a simple cog they could twist and turn as they wanted.

The Oligarchs had been warned:

You can keep your billions.

But stay out of my way . . .

CHAPTER TWO

Six Years Earlier

June 7, 1994, 5:00 p.m.,

Logovaz Club, 40 Novokuznetskaya Street, Moscow

Forty-eight years old, dark hair thinning above bright, buoyant features, Boris Abramovich Berezovsky had the unique ability to appear to be moving, even on the rare occasions when he was standing still. In his more usual state—rushing from one meeting to the next, compact shoulders hunched low over his diminutive body—he was an ambition-fueled bullet train emancipated from its tracks, a frantic dervish of arms and legs.

Bursting out into the covered rear security entrance of his company's headquarters, a renovated nineteenth-century mansion situated halfway down a tree-lined private road in an upscale section of Moscow, every molecule beneath Berezovsky's skin seemed to vibrate, as one hand straightened his suit jacket over his pressed white shirt, while his pinpoint eyes navigated the few feet that separated him from his waiting limousine. As usual, the gleaming Mercedes-Benz 600 was parked as close to the door as possible, so that the overhanging concrete eaves provided ample cover. If that wasn't enough, there was also the hulking bodyguard standing beside the open rear door of the automobile, as well as the driver, nodding through the reinforced front windshield.

The car was already running. Berezovsky was a businessman, and in Russia in the mid-1990s, it wasn't good business for a man in his position to spend more time than necessary going between office and car. Even here, on his home turf, behind the pre-Revolution manor that he'd painstakingly restored to a state of opulence—lavish interior filled with expensive furniture, impeccably dressed attendants, even an oversize aquarium running along one wall—he had to be cautious.

He kept his gaze low as he hurried toward the car. The covered security entrance was designed to ensure the privacy of those who most needed it; since the entrance was essentially enclosed, it would be impossible for a stray passerby to stroll close enough to see anything. But even if somehow someone had wandered inside the security entrance in time to watch Berezovsky give an officious wink toward the bodyguard and slide his minute form into the backseat of the Mercedes, the pedestrian would have known to look away quickly. Berezovsky wasn't particularly famous, but he emanated power—from his expensive suit to his frenetic pace. Those who did recognize him might have described him as an entrepreneur. They might have called him a vastly successful car salesman, or a former academic who had turned to finance. All of these things were true—and all of them were laughably insufficient. Even those who knew him well could only hope to scrape the surface of what he was—and the heights toward which his ambition was driving him.

Safely ensconced in the interior of the car, Berezovsky waited for the bodyguard to join the driver up front. Then the car immediately started forward.

Berezovsky tried to relax as the Mercedes navigated away from the curb and entered the sparse, late-afternoon traffic. It was hard for him to believe it was only Tuesday. It had been a long week already. The past forty-eight hours had been filled with meetings, mostly with executives from AvtoVAZ—Russia's largest car maker, known mostly for its signature automobile, the boxy, functional Lada, affectionately dubbed "the people's car"—and with Berezovsky's underlings at LogoVAZ. He'd formed the company five years ago, originally to supply AvtoVAZ's computer software, but it had evolved into Russia's largest Lada dealership, with showrooms all over the country. Those forty-eight hours had been full of banal conversations, only made bearable by the sumptuousness of the setting, his Logovaz Club. No matter how busy things got, Berezovsky often made sure that the last appointment of each day took place in the private apartment he kept on the top floor of his headquarters, where a stunning, young girlfriend might keep his top shelf vodka poured and waiting.

Though the meetings had dragged on, and as tedious as the subject matter had been, it was the time between each assignation that Berezovsky hated most. That was why most of his business took place at the club, where he could quickly pirouette between appointments, losing mere seconds in transit. Going off-site meant dealing with the necessary delays of the outside world—traffic, physical distance, the whims and inefficiencies of other people's schedules. It wasn't just Berezovsky's internal wiring that made him miserable at the thought of wasted minutes—the fact that he couldn't sit still, even with his back against the most luxurious leather that Mercedes could manufacture—it was the knowledge of how valuable every lost minute could be. To him, the Breguet on his wrist didn't measure time; it kept track of lost opportunities.

Berezovsky was well aware that this impatience was yet another symptom of the seismic shift that had engulfed his world, beginning less than a decade earlier. Impatience, ambition, the ability to dream big and live even bigger—none of these things had mattered in the Russia of his childhood. The best a young, mathematically gifted Jewish kid from Moscow, with no connections among the Communist elite and no knowledge of the outside world, could have hoped for was a doctorate in mathematics from one of the few universities that accepted the less desirable ethnicities. No matter how many awards he'd gone on to win, or papers he'd published, he'd been heading toward a simple, quiet life of books and laboratories.

And then—*Perestroika*, the lightning bolt that had shattered everything. First, the old world fell in fits and bouts to Gorbachev and, rising parallel to him, Yeltsin. Then a chaotic new world haphazardly emerged, buoyed by an infant form of capitalism that was just now reaching its chaotic teenage years.

Suddenly a man who was good with numbers, could think theoretically and far enough ahead not to get bogged down in the absurdities of the nearly lawless moment—and light enough on his feet to dance over the inevitable aftershocks of a science-fiction-level restructuring of an entire nation from the ground up—suddenly, such a man had a chance at a brand-new future. Being different, being an outsider, the very qualities that had impeded success in a world built behind walls, were a form of insulation when those walls came crashing down.

Berezovsky hadn't wasted a moment wondering what would come next. He'd turned his attention toward a world where money suddenly had meaning. That, in turn, had led him to what he earnestly believed to be the holiest relic of this new, free, capitalist system his country hoped to become.

Berezovsky grinned as he ran his gaze over the parked cars flashing by on either side of his limousine. Aside from the odd foreign model—mostly German, like his Mercedes, or almost as frequently Japanese, Toyotas and Hondas—the majority of the cars they passed were Ladas. Squat, compact, rugged, and without a hint of glamour or wasted expense, each Lada represented the culmination of a previously unimaginable dream. Perestroika or not, a Muscovite didn't simply wake up after 1991 with a pile of rubles under his bed, ready to stroll to the nearest car dealership.

In truth, the Lada had become the first symbol of the new, free Russia. Owning a Lada was everything, and to get one a person needed more than money. You also needed knowledge of the right person to bribe.

Berezovsky hadn't set his sights on owning a Lada; he'd set his sights on the company that made them. Initially, he'd worked with the skill set he'd acquired in his academic life; he'd founded Logo-VAZ as a computer software company aimed at solving numerical payment issues for the newly accountable auto conglomerate.

Working his way deeper into the sprawling corporate behemoth, he'd quickly realized that the men who'd been placed in charge of AvtoVAZ were functionaries of the old world: dinosaurs who didn't understand the economic changes exploding around them. These Red Directors, as the history books would eventually label them, had been handed the reins of major companies across every industry by a government that itself hardly understood the capitalist world that perestroika had unleashed.

In the back of the Mercedes, Berezovsky's attention settled on a pair of Ladas parked next to each other in the driveway of a two-story office supply company a few buildings down from his headquarters. He could envision it all in his head, the journey those automobiles had taken to get into that driveway. Birthed on an assembly line in the vast manufacturing plant on the banks of the Volga river, then a lengthy trek via barge and truck to the urban centers where the buying public lived; on to guarded dealer lots, where the cars would be briefly stored before finding their way into a showroom. And then the final transaction itself, rubles changing hands, usually through a "connected" middleman—along with a silent prayer that the seeds of cash would somehow bear automotive fruit.

So much distance traveled, so much time wasted: but in this situation, Berezovsky had realized, they weren't simply minutes to be mourned. These were minutes to be *utilized*. The Americans had a saying, born of capitalism: time is money. Berezovsky had made his first fortune off the literal application of that cliché.

Berezovsky's Mercedes slipped past the driveway and the pair of Ladas, then worked its way by another row of parked cars—a Toyota, a handful of older AvtoVAZ models, then a dust-covered German-made Opel, squatting directly in front of a curbside fruit stand. Berezovsky didn't spend a lot of time thinking about his past, but it still gave him pleasure to remember the scheme that had first put him on the map. It wasn't something he would have talked about in an interview, nor was it something an interviewer would ever have dared ask him about. Even so, he was quite proud of the simple elegance of his first real venture.

Manufacturing line to consumer, an incredible journey of miles and minutes: these had been the perfect ingredients for an epic level of arbitrage. In the free-fall economy of Russia's teenage capitalism, time was usually considered an enemy to money. Double- and triple-digit inflation had turned every ruble into a rapidly leaking balloon, shrinking by the second. But Berezovsky had been able to turn this enemy to his advantage. He had come up with a scheme to take a large number of cars on consignment, paying the Red Directors only a nominal down payment, which, for the most part, they had happily pocketed. Then Berezovsky sold the cars through his various dealerships. After that, he'd wait months—or even years—to make good on the balance of what he owed AvtoVAZ, letting inflation do its work. By the time he'd paid off his debt, he was putting down kopecks on the ruble. In short order, Logovaz was earning more than six hundred percent profit on every car it sold.

And that had only been the beginning. Berezovsky had built on his reputation as the premier Lada dealer to open a banking fund to pre-order even more cars. He'd raised almost sixty million dollars toward that end—money he was in no rush to turn over to AvtoVAZ, or anyone else.

Perhaps the most incredible thing about his venture was that none of what he was doing was technically illegal. It was simply arbitrage, a mathematical and ambitious mind taking advantage of an inefficiency in an existing market. Of course, the fact that Berezovsky hadn't broken any explicit laws didn't mean he hadn't ruffled any feathers. The car business, like every other business in modern Russia, existed in a chaotic vacuum many people liked to call the Wild East. Where there was money to be made, there were often men with guns involved. Almost daily, the Russian newspapers had reported stories of businessmen murdered because of deals gone bad.

To Berezovsky, the dangerous elements on the fringes of the business world were simply an unfortunate cost of this new, free market. Successful corporations adapted, dedicating resources to defend themselves against what they called "wet work," perhaps an overly graphic term for the assassination trade, borrowed from the world of organized crime. Rumor was, Logovaz had outsourced its wet work to a team of "specialists"—a murky association about which Berezovsky wanted to know as little as possible. Even so, his dealerships had not been immune to the violence. A few of his showrooms had even been shot up over the past few weeks, though nobody had been killed. Even more frightening, a known member of a powerful Russian gangland outfit had recently approached Berezovsky himself, demanding the resolution of some unimportant difference of opinion. Berezovsky had essentially waved the man away—and, a few days later, there had been a pitched gun battle outside one of his regional Lada showrooms. A half dozen unclaimed Chechen and Russian bodies were carted off by the local police.

Bulletproof limousines, high-priced bodyguards, paid mercenaries: business as usual under perestroika. Unpleasant but necessary, and the furthest thing from Berezovsky's thoughts as he watched the parked cars flashing by. His mind shifted ahead to the dinner he was about to attend; more deals to be made, more rubles to be mined out of minutes. After dinner, he would take the short ride back to his club—and maybe arrange a visit to the upstairs apartment. As his Mercedes moved alongside the dust-covered Opel, he was imagining the smell of perfume, curves shifting beneath sheets. And then, entirely by accident, Berezovsky noticed something odd out of the corner of his vision. It might have been nothing at all— maybe a trick of light against the bulletproof window to his left, or even a shadow from the high fruit stand that rose up behind the parked car. But he thought he saw a wisp of dark smoke coming out of the Opel's trunk.

He opened his mouth to say something to his driver—but before the words could come out, there was a sudden flash of light.

And then the shock wave hit.

The Mercedes was lifted three feet off the ground, tilting sickeningly in the air. The window to Berezovsky's left exploded inward, jagged shards of bulletproof glass pelting his face, neck, and shoulder. He felt a brief moment of weightlessness—and then the limo crashed back to the ground, both axles snapping from the force. The sound came next, a howling roar loud enough to pop both his eardrums, hitting him like a fist against his skull, slamming him back against the warping leather seat.

And then the heat. His eyes went wide as a ball of searing flame engulfed his entire world, bright orange licks of fire clawing at the exposed skin of his face, neck, and hands. He screamed, slapping at the pain, then found himself rolling forward, almost by instinct. The next thing he knew, his knees and hands hit pavement, and he was crawling through broken glass. A strange scent, acrid and sweet at the same time, filled his nostrils; he realized it was the scent of his own skin burning. He screamed again, lurching forward on the glass-covered road, away from the heat. Finally, he was able to lift himself to his feet.

He turned back toward his car—and stared at the burning, mangled mess of metal. It took him a full minute to understand what he was seeing; much of the chassis was melted right into the pavement, the windows were all blown out, the outer fuselage warped beyond recognition. He shifted his attention to the front seat. His bodyguard wasn't visible, but he could see his driver, still sitting behind what was left of the steering wheel. The man looked strange, hunched forward at an odd angle, smoke rising from his jacket. Berezovsky was about to call out to him—when he came to a sudden realization.

The man no longer had a head.

Berezovsky collapsed to his knees, as sirens sang in the distance.

CHAPTER THREE

June 8, 1994, 2:00 a.m.,

Logovaz Club

"**W**ELL, THIS IS NEW."

Alexander Litvinenko ran his fingers through his hair, as he watched Igor Davny, a junior agent under his command, trying to pry what appeared to be a piece of a leather seat cushion from the base of a partially melted, steel trash can. The leather had fused to the steel, making the task nearly impossible, but Davny wasn't going to give up so easily. The young man cursed as his gloved hands slipped off the material, then he bent at the waist for another go.

"Now they're blowing each other up," Davny continued, with a grunt of effort, as he worked on the leather. "Less efficient than a bullet, but I guess it makes a statement."

Litvinenko grimaced, refusing to see the humor in the situation. It was the middle of the night, and he had much better things to do than pick through a still-smoldering crime scene. As a newly promoted officer on the central staff of the FSB, the Federal Security Service of the Russian Federation, specializing in counterterrorism and organized crime, he had thought he was beyond this sort of menial task. When he had gotten the emergency call, he had just crawled into bed with his new girlfriend—Marina, a ballroom dancer, twice as beautiful as he deserved—after a long dinner at a friend's house.

He took great care as he stepped over a piece of wood from the nearby destroyed fruit stand. They were still a good ten yards from the center of the blast radius, but even here, the air was thick with the scent of ash, burning pavement, and melted rubber.

He shifted his gaze toward the spot next to the mangled Mercedes limousine at the direct center of the crime scene, where the most senior investigators were crawling through a pile of rubble and shrapnel—the remains of the parked Opel, or ground zero, as the inevitable report would declare. Litvinenko was already certain what the investigators would find; he'd surveyed the blast area when he'd first arrived on the scene. A fairly sophisticated explosive device, hidden in a parked car. The bomb had been detonated by remote, and despite what the younger agent might have thought, this wasn't a unique crime scene at all. Litvinenko was well aware, from his latest officer's briefing, that over the past few days, there had been at least two other bombings in Moscow—one of them right in front of the Tchaikovsky Concert Hall. Both had been "business related"—and considering the most likely target of this evening's attack, this incident was of a similar nature.

If anything, this explosion was the mildest of the three. There had been surprisingly few casualties, considering the size of the bomb, and the brazen location and timing of the detonation—the middle of the afternoon, just a few doors down from the Logovaz Club.

"He's one lucky bastard," Davny said, finally giving up on the strip of leather. The young agent moved next to Litvinenko, likewise scanning the crime scene in front of them. "Burns to his hands and face, some shrapnel wounds, but other than that, nothing serious."

"His driver wasn't quite as lucky," Litvinenko noted.

The man's head had been sheared right off by a chunk of the Opel's trunk. The force of the explosion had been severe; aside from the mangled Mercedes, at least five other cars had been utterly destroyed, along with the fruit stand and eight stories of windows of an office building across the street. Amazingly, only six pedestrians had been injured, and only the decapitated driver had left the scene in a body bag.

Well, two body bags.

Davny was right, Berezovsky had been damn lucky. The burns would heal, the shrapnel would be removed. According to Litvinenko's higher-ups, the auto mogul was planning on heading to a sanitarium in Switzerland to recoup and recover. LogoVAZ had already released a statement to the press about the attack, which Litvinenko had read on the ride over to the crime scene:

"There are simply very powerful forces in this society which seek to hinder the creation of civilized business and the revival of the economy. And they will use barbarian, criminal methods to get what they want. It is hard to fight."

Succinct, accurate—and more than a little hypocritical. *Civilized business.* Three years of FSB work investigating organized crime, three years before that working under the Third Chief Directorate of the KGB, the main security service of the Soviet Union until its collapse in 1991: Litvinenko had become an expert on the way business was usually conducted in his home country, and *civilized* was about the last word he would have chosen to describe what he'd seen. Then again, the security services—not to mention the military bureaucracy, and, hell, the entire goddamn government—weren't exactly bastions of virtue, and never had been. The KGB, the pre-Gorbachev Soviet machinery—at least back then, you knew what to expect. You kept your head down, did what you were supposed to do, and usually you came out okay. Now? Often, Litvinenko felt as lost as the youngest of his underlings.

In his opinion, the FSB was a shadow of its precursor. Certainly, if his dwindling paycheck was any indication, the "revival of the economy" was going a lot better for the "civilized businessmen" blowing each other up in Mercedes limousines than for the men charged with keeping tabs on the mayhem.

Litvinenko knew that many of his colleagues had been taking things into their own hands—moonlighting for companies and wealthy businessmen, heading up security organizations, using their specific skills to take part in the new economy. Technically, it was illegal, and an agent could get fired—or even arrested—for taking part in after-hours corporate work. But usually, the higher-ups looked the other way. For the most part, turning a blind eye to indiscretions had become a way of life for the bureaucrats who were, themselves, trying to navigate through a world that now seemed constantly in flux. It was only under very special circumstances that the people in power focused their attention on any one individual or incident. Usually, that sort of focus could only mean trouble—for everyone involved.

Litvinenko concentrated on the scene in front of him, shifting his gaze outward from the center—the mangled limousine, hunched forward like a dying jungle beast on two broken axles, surrounded by a lake of broken glass and melted asphalt—to the outer rings of the shock wave, nearly twenty yards in every direction. Across the scene, he counted at least a dozen investigators, working their way through the rubble with plastic evidence bags and shiny forceps.

Davny waved a gloved hand.

"All this because someone tried to murder a car salesman."

This time, Litvinenko laughed. He didn't know if his young charge was serious or not, but Boris Berezovsky was obviously much more than a car salesman. The very fact that Litvinenko had been dragged out here in the middle of the night to personally take part in the investigation was evidence of that. Although Litvinenko was hazy on the details, he had heard that the request for special attention had come all the way from the top. Apparently, this Berezovsky had some sort of connection to Yeltsin himself. Litvinenko hadn't asked any questions when the assignment had come down, and he certainly wouldn't have gotten any answers from his direct superiors at the FSB.

"It isn't murder when you blow up an entire street to try to kill one man."

"So that's what happened here?" Davny asked. "An assassination attempt?"

Litvinenko gently kicked with his leather boot at a piece of singed wood from the destroyed fruit stand.

"What happened here, comrade, is Mr. Berezovsky's roof fell in."

Davny looked at him, then finally nodded, because he understood. Litvinenko wasn't talking about the fruit stand.

Krysha—literally, roof—was a uniquely Russian concept. Originally, the term had its roots in the world of organized crime; gangsters were only as powerful as their "roof"—the person or organization that protected them in case things went awry. The form of protection a "roof" might offer could be physical, economic, political, or even personal; although the concept was often loaded with the threat of real violence, the most effective forms of krysha never had to resort to guns and bombs. An implication of threat was often far more chilling than when pressure was applied.

In the realm of business, the concept of krysha—a protective roof—was no different, but without the essential criminal link. The Red Directors who had at first inherited the newly privatized companies of the ex-Soviet regime had, some might argue, the ultimate roof—a government that would protect them as long as they stayed in favor. Private businessmen—men like Berezovsky—needed a different sort of roof to protect them as they chased their ambitions. Increasingly, these businessmen were turning to the very organizations that had coined the term, with varying results.

"Chechens?" Davny asked. "Russians? Georgians?"

Litvinenko shrugged. Of course, it could have been either. All three territories had extensive networks of organized crime. All of them had a reputation for being particularly vicious and violent; but for the right price, there were plenty of gangs willing to take up the cause of "civilized business."

Lately there had been a rash of business-related incidents: numerous gun battles in city streets, shootouts in restaurants and office buildings. Even a case of chemical poisoning, involving the toxic heavy metal cadmium, placed on the rim of a banker's coffee cup. And now, apparently, car bombs.

Litvinenko had no idea who Boris Berezovsky had pissed off to get himself on someone's shit list, but he was certain that the crime scene in front of them was the result of a business disagreement. Someone was testing the strength of Berezovsky's roof. From the files Litvinenko's superiors had given him on the way over to the site, he knew that Berezovsky had an associate, a partner in his LogoVAZ corporation, a Georgian strongman named Badri Patarkatsishvili, who, if not connected to the types of people who could provide a roof for a growing business, could talk the sort of language such people would understand. But it was obvious that Berezovsky and his Georgian strongman didn't have access to the kind of roof that kept you safe forever.

"Whoever it was, I think they got their point across."

Litvinenko kicked at the heat-darkened pavement beneath his boots. He wasn't concerned with keeping the crime scene pristine; he knew full well that he wasn't going to find any answers picking through the smoldering dirt. Besides, he wasn't entirely certain he wanted answers, no matter how connected this Berezovsky might be. *Look too hard,* he thought to himself, *and you ran the risk of finding something.*

In the world he was living in now, wasn't it better to simply turn a blind eye?

He exhaled, thinking about his beautiful ballroom dancer. Then his gaze shifted back to the mangled Mercedes limousine.

What sort of life could a man like him make for himself in this new Russia?

What sort of roof did *he* have?

CHAPTER FOUR

November 1994,

42 Kosygin Street,

Vorobyovy Gory (Sparrow Hills), Moscow

T HE BIG MAN IN the towel was moving fast, steam coming off his thick, bare shoulders in violent plumes as his pawlike feet left wet prints on the hardwood floor. He was surprisingly agile for a man his size. Two steps behind him, Berezovsky was breathing hard trying to keep up. It wasn't until the gargantuan finally slowed in front of a bank of lockers in a quiet corner of the dressing room, that Berezovsky could be certain that the man was even listening to him.

Berezovsky had been engaged in a one-sided conversation with the man's back for most of the morning, traveling through half the Presidential Club along the way—from the tennis courts to the steam room, past the movie theater and the dining room, even through the showers. Well aware of the absurd spectacle they cut on their journey through the club, and not merely because of the difference in their sizes, Berezovsky could hear the whispers of the politicians and dignitaries they had passed along the way; the bandages on his arms and head were hard to ignore, and he knew that the boldest of the club's members had even begun referring to him as Smoky. But to Berezovsky, it wasn't an insult; he wore his burns as a badge.

The very fact that he had survived the car bombing five months ago marked him as special. By all accounts, he should have died. The explosion that had destroyed his car and killed his driver should have cooked him like a potato wrapped in foil. The FSB agent in charge of the investigation—Alexander "Sasha" Litvinenko, a man Berezovsky found surprisingly sincere—had told him that he actually owed his life to the incompetence of his poor decapitated former employee. His driver had forgotten to lock the car doors when he'd pulled away from the curb; otherwise, Berezovsky would never have gotten out of that burning vehicle.

Berezovsky had spent ten days on his back in a Swiss sanitarium, recovering from his burns and contemplating his place in the world. By the end of his stay, he had come to an important decision: simply being a businessman in modern Russia was no longer enough. In Russia, the walls didn't hold up the roof; the roof kept the walls from falling in. Without a strong roof, no matter how lavish your house, it would eventually come down.

Which was why, now, almost six months later, he had been spending nearly every day at the Presidential Club. The sprawling complex—Boris Yeltsin's pride and joy, which he had modeled after a sporting resort he had once visited in the Urals—was much more than an adult playground. From the steam rooms to the indoor tennis courts, these were the true halls of power in the Yeltsin administration. You wanted to get something done, you didn't go to the Kremlin—you grabbed a tennis racket and booked a court.

Berezovsky continued the monologue he'd been engaged in for the better part of the morning. As the large man in front of him traded his towel for a tailored white shirt and gray slacks, he said,

"So, you see, it makes sense from a political perspective. It truly isn't about the money."

The man rolled his eyes as he went to work on the buttons of his shirt.

"Boris, I'm not a fool. With you, it is always about the money."

Berezovsky smiled, though there was a bitter taste in his mouth. He knew what Alexander Vasilyevich Korzhakov really thought of him; not dislike, exactly, but pity. To Korzhakov, Berezovsky was a weak little man covered in bandages, a glorified car salesman. But Berezovsky also knew that, as much as Korzhakov pitied and ridiculed him, he couldn't ignore him.

Berezovsky was the only businessman who was an official member of the Presidential Club, and he had been invited to join just days after the assassination attempt, his burns still visible on his arms and face.

"Eventually, yes," Berezovsky conceded. "There will be money. But that's beside the point."

Korzhakov laughed. "So you are going to run a TV station?"

It did sound crazy set out in the open, so succinctly; he had built his fortune in cars. But now it wasn't simply a fortune he was after. The changes he intended to make in his life meant he needed to branch into businesses that would give him power as well as cash. And for days now, he had been pummeling Korzhakov with his most recent inspiration.

"Me? I'm a car salesman. But I'm certain that together, we can find someone who knows how to work a television camera."

Korzhakov grunted, but Berezovsky could see the calculations beginning behind the man's eyes. Berezovsky did not consider Korzhakov his intellectual equal, not by a long shot; but the man had a certain animal intelligence that Berezovsky had to admire. His current status was evidence enough. If the rumors were true, Korzhakov was more than just an access point into the Yeltsin government. The president's health had been fading for quite some time, and the vacuum of power was at least partially being filled by the slab of a man pulling on his pants in front of Berezovsky.

The simplest description of Alexander Korzhakov was that he was Boris Yeltsin's bodyguard. Since 1987, when he'd left his post in the KGB—forcibly retired, if some reports were to be believed, for his "liberal" leanings—he had been protecting Yeltsin, running a well-armed security team that now numbered in the hundreds. He had been by Yeltsin's side for no fewer than two coup attempts—and he knew exactly how close Yeltsin's government had come to falling. In 1991, when hard-line Communists with tanks had attempted to retake Moscow, it was Yeltsin who had climbed atop one of the tanks, like a white-haired beacon of freedom, rallying the people behind him; but it was Korzhakov who had helped the already ailing president onto the iron vehicle, climbing right up beside him for all the photographers to see. And in 1993, when Yeltsin had ordered the storming of the Russian White House to protect the fledgling government from the right-wing politicians who had been trying to forcibly turn back the clock to Communism, Korzhakov had again been by the president's side. This time it was Yeltsin who had controlled the tanks: parking them in the center of the city, firing at the government building until it was reduced to rubble.

Certainly, over the past ten years, Korzhakov had earned Yeltsin's trust—and, more important, his ear.

"Alexander Vasilyevich," Berezovksy said, lowering his voice so the larger man had to lean in to hear him. "Moving forward, it isn't tanks that will keep our democracy alive."

"Again, we are back to money."

Berezovsky shrugged.

"Money, but more important than money—media."

Korzhakov ran the towel over what was left of his hair.

"Ah, yes. You and your hippie newspaperman are going to save Mother Russia."

Berezovsky smiled, though he knew there was at least a tinge of venom behind the bodyguard's words. *Your hippie newspaperman.* The description might have been used in a derogatory manner, but that didn't make it any less accurate.

Berezovsky's entrance into Yeltsin's inner circle and, indeed, the Presidential Club—had been the result of much strategy and choreography, the core of which had revolved around Korzhakov's "hippie newspaperman," a journalist named Valentin Yumashev. The young man—shy, handsome, and usually poorly attired—had been working at a liberal, youth-skewed political magazine—which Berezovsky's LogoVAZ had funded as a location to place car ads. Berezovksy had always thought that the man's talents were being wasted writing articles about democracy aimed at teenagers.

The opportunity to use Yumashev's skills for something more worthwhile had presented itself about a year ago, when he had been hired as a writer to pen the president's autobiography after interviewing President Yeltsin for an article. Seeking a publisher for the book, Yumashev had eventually approached Berezovsky, who had realized that his involvement as publisher would bring him closer to Yeltsin and give him some level of entrance into the halls of political power.

Even better, Yeltsin had immediately taken to the writer on a personal level—and, yet more significant was that Yeltsin's youngest daughter, Tatiana, had struck up a relationship with the handsome Yumashev. Almost instantly, Berezovsky was able to ride upward with

Yumashev's fortune, and went from being an outsider to part of Yeltsin's inner circle—a group of influence known outside the Kremlin as the Family. A man like Korzhakov—a product of the old world, a former KGB general who had made his bones in the military—might have blanched at the sight of a businessman and a twentysomething writer ascending so quickly into Yeltsin's orbit, but there was little he could do. He mocked Berezovsky behind his back—but he had no choice but to listen when Berezovsky spoke long and loud enough.

And this idea—this golden idea—was something Berezovsky knew was worth speaking about until his throat—or the bodyguard—gave out.

"We aren't talking about newspapers, Alexander Vasilyevich."

Korzhakov waved a meaty hand.

"Right, your television station. As if we don't have enough trouble with Gusinsky and his pornography as it is."

Berezovsky stifled the urge to spit.

"Gusinsky's swill is the exact opposite of what I'm proposing."

It was obvious that Korzhakov knew he'd hit a nerve, and his eyes told Berezovsky he was enjoying the moment.

On paper, the two Oligarchs, Gusinsky and Berezovsky, appeared to be cut from the same cloth—both were from Jewish backgrounds, both had risen from obscurity to great financial wealth by taking advantage of perestroika. But the mere mention of the rival businessman's name made Berezovsky's scars twitch beneath his bandages.

Whereas Berezovsky had taken a roundabout route to his fortune, exploiting the inefficiencies in the car market, Gusinsky had taken a more direct approach, building a banking conglomerate with the help and protection of Moscow's Mayor's office. Once the coffers of Most Bank had made Gusinsky immensely wealthy, he had turned his attentions to the media, building an independent television station to rival the state-owned network—which, while a ratings behemoth, was still a clunky remnant of the Communist era. Gusinsky's NTV might not have actually manufactured pornography, but its quest for popularity had led to programming that had ruffled feathers in the administration, especially when it had begun airing programs that took a critical view of Russia's recent involvement in the Chechen conflict.

"NTV is little more than a nuisance," Berezovsky continued. "I'm talking about a real television network. ORT."

Korzhakov raised an eyebrow. *Общественное Российское Телевидение* Russian Public Television, the state-owned network, dwarfed Gusinsky's startup. In fact, with almost two hundred million daily viewers, it was bigger than all the American networks combined. It was also leaking money, losing almost a quarter billion dollars a year. And, as everyone knew, it was one of the most corrupt institutions in modern Russia.

"You want the president to give you ORT?"

It was a blunt way of wording things, but Korzhakov had always been a blunt instrument. The truth was, Berezovsky had not invented the concept of privatization. The planned economy had vanished—and something needed to take its place. Privatization, the idea of taking companies away from the state and essentially handing them to financiers and businessmen, was technically the brainchild of an economist named Anatoly Chubais, a brilliant young deputy in the Yeltsin government. It had begun as a noble idea—a way to offer the nation's resources directly to the people, in the form of vouchers that acted as stock certificates. But the voucher program had failed almost immediately, a victim of the massive inflation that had helped make Berezovsky so wealthy.

This had led to a shift, from a voucher program aimed at the common man to options sold to the only people who had enough money left to purchase them—the small group of businessmen who had taken an early advantage in the new economy. The more desperate the government became to fund itself through Chubais's program, the more leverage the Oligarchs attained. When one of the largest oil companies in the nation went into a privatization auction, a company valued at many billions of dollars ended up selling for close to two hundred fifty million. Timber, copper, automobiles, textiles—one after another, Russia's major industries ended up in the hands of a small group of like-minded businessmen.

"You've got it backwards, Alexander Vasilyevich. I want to hand ORT to the president."

Korzhakov looked at him, those blunt gears turning behind his gaze. In two years there would be another election; Korzhakov knew as well as anyone how fragile the fledgling government was. Having the nation's largest television network in Yeltsin's pocket might very well make the difference. *And if it didn't?* Well, there were always more tanks.

Berezovsky began to lay out his plan. He and a group of colleagues would put up enough cash to buy forty-nine percent of ORT at auction, leaving the government in charge of the majority fifty-one percent. They would use the network to prop up Yeltsin's democratic ideals, everything building toward the 1996 campaign. Everyone was going to come out a winner.

Almost everyone.

"I can imagine how your friend Gusinsky is going to react."

Berezovsky shrugged.

"Perhaps he will understand, it's simply good business and good politics. Or perhaps he can be made to understand."

Korzhakov didn't respond. This was not the first time Berezovsky had discussed Gusinsky in such terms; at some point in the past, he might even have used the word *terminate* in casual conversation. Always, Korzhakov, who had fired mortars at the Russian White House, brushed away his suggestions. Berezovsky saw no distinction between a political rival and a business rival. Both could have a change of heart when looking down the barrel of a gun.

Sooner or later, Korzhakov would recognize Gusinsky—with the Moscow mayor in his pocket—as the adversary he truly was. If not, Berezovsky was prepared to go over the bodyguard's head. Other members of the Family would be receptive. Tatiana and Yumashev could convince Tatiana's father, if Korzhakov refused. After all, according to the rumors, Gusinsky had already built a private army of heavily armed bodyguards—some said over a thousand strong—stationed near and around Media-Most's building in the heart of Moscow. Gusinsky was formidable, with the support of the mayor of the biggest city in Russia; but a mayor wasn't the same as a president.

"ORT," Korzhakov mused. "A little bit of business, a lot of politics. How you've changed, Boris. And all it took was a bomb going off next to your car."

Then he jabbed his thick paw toward the bandages covering part of Berezovsky's scalp.

"You don't exactly have a face for TV."

Berezovsky smiled, but, inside, his mathematical mind was already churning forward. It wasn't *his* face that two hundred million people needed to fall in love with; he wasn't the one running for president.

"Let me worry about the business," he said. "You take care of the politics."

Before either of these things, Berezovsky thought to himself, there was a goose that needed hunting.

CHAPTER FIVE

December 2, 1994, 11:00 a.m.,

36 Novy Arbat Street, Moscow

"**N**OW IT'S FOUR. DEFINITELY four. Twenty yards back, the gray Mercedes. Since about six miles ago."

Anton Gogol felt his fingers whiten against the steering wheel. He tried to keep his voice steady and professional, but his insides were growing tighter with each passing second. He could tell that his colleague seated next to him in the passenger seat was equally disturbed. Though eight years his senior, the "security specialist" made no effort to hide the trembling of his fingers as he slid a double-barreled shotgun out from beneath his seat and placed it gingerly on his lap.

Then he nodded toward the rearview mirror.

"And the other three? They've been with us since the dacha?"

"Nearly that long."

Ivan Doctorow nodded, then spoke quietly into the transponder in his upper jacket pocket. Anton had no doubt that the bodyguards in the other two cars of their motorcade were already aware of the tailing vehicles. If anything, Anton was the least experienced among them, having joined their unit just a year ago—and only three years after he'd finished his training service with the now defunct KGB. Then again, he doubted that any amount of training would have prepared him for the situation that was rapidly developing around them.

When Anton's motorcade had left his employer's country home forty minutes ago, there had been no indication that this would be anything more than a routine trip to the office. A blustery, snowy Friday in December, the sky the same gunmetal hue as the barrels of the shotgun that now sat on his partner's lap. Anton had made this drive countless times in the past year, sometimes in the lead car, now fifteen yards ahead of him on the multilane highway, sometimes seated in the driver's seat right in front of his employer—separated from the Oligarch by a deceptively thin sheet of smoked Plexiglas. He usually preferred the trail car, as it involved a relatively simple set of expectations. One eye on the taillights of the bulletproof limousine at the center of the motorcade, the rest of his attention on the rearview mirror and the highway behind them. Even in these turbulent times, a well-armed motorcade was enough to discourage even the most brazen of threats. On top of that, Anton's employer's reputation—and the small army he had built himself—had insulated him from the troubles of many of his peers.

Which made the current situation all the more concerning.

"FSB? Some subset of the local police?" Anton asked.

Ivan shrugged.

"Unmarked cars, foreign make. The windows are too tinted to see if they are wearing uniforms."

"How does he want to handle this?"

Ivan showed no emotion beyond the slight tremor in his hands as he listened to the piece in his right ear.

"It's only another few miles to the office. Middle of the day, major highway at rush hour. Nobody would be foolish enough to try something here."

Anton nodded, though he could taste the bile rising in his throat. He wasn't going to question his more experienced partner, but he certainly read the morning newspapers. His boss hadn't hired half a platoon of ex-KGB men because he was hoping to fix a parking ticket.

They continued on in silence, Anton trying to focus on his employer's limousine. For all he knew, there were sniper rifles now trained at the back of his head. He reminded himself that the rear windshield was bulletproof, and that it was extremely difficult to hit a target from a moving vehicle. Neither thought gave him much comfort.

Thankfully, after another excruciating few minutes, he caught sight of the off-white, high-rise headquarters in the near distance; the impressive complex was hard to miss, towering over a huge parking lot and the multilane highway. Just the sight of the building took some of the tension out of Anton's body. As the first cars in his motorcade turned off the highway and into the parking area, Anton had to keep himself from pressing too hard on the gas. The last thing he wanted to do was overtake his employer's limousine. Still, he couldn't stifle the beginnings of a smile—until he noticed that Ivan, in the seat next to him, had turned a sickly shade of gray.

Anton looked again into the rearview mirror—the four un-marked cars had also turned off the highway, drawing to a stop next to one another in the far corner of the parking lot. Anton exhaled. If the people following them had simply been trying to scare them, they would have remained on the highway.

Anton's colleagues in the other two cars had obviously noticed the odd behavior as well. Without warning the lead car suddenly accelerated, tires spitting smoke as the vehicle tore toward the front entrance of the office building. His employer's limousine followed right behind, and Anton acted without thought, his foot suddenly heavy against the gas. The roar of his engine nearly drowned out the squeal of rubber against asphalt.

Three seconds later, all three cars screeched to a halt in front of the front glass entrance to the building. A half dozen bodyguards fanned out onto the sidewalk, forming a wedge around the limousine. Another second, and the Oligarch was out of the car and being hustled into the building. The glass doors locked behind him. And then—nothing.

Anton waited, engine running. Ivan was still clutching the shotgun while speaking into his transponder. At the response, he nodded. Then he looked back through the rearview window at the four unmarked cars. A light snow had begun to fall, inching up around their tires.

"Calls are being made," Ivan said. "Nobody seems to know who they are. Interior Ministry, Moscow police, the tax office. Our security chief has reached the FSB. They are sending officers to investigate."

"So we wait?" Anton asked.

Ivan didn't bother to answer. The only sound was the soft patter of snow against the roof of the car.

It was an hour at least before a sleek, black, Russian-made sedan with official FSB plates pulled into the parking lot behind them and headed directly to a spot a half dozen yards from the four unmarked cars.

Anton watched as two uniformed agents exited the sedan and crossed toward the closest of the mysterious cars. Before the men had gone half the distance, the rear doors of the foreign car opened and three men exited. Anton's entire body tensed up as he took in the military-grade flak jackets and camouflage vests. The vests bore no insignia. More startling, all three men were wearing black balaclavas and sporting submachine guns slung over their shoulders.

The two FSB officers froze in their tracks. One of them said something to the three men, which evoked only laughter. Then, without warning, one of the three strangers casually pointed his submachine gun at the two FSB men. The FSB men shouted something—then turned and moved quickly back to their car. A moment later, they had slammed the car doors behind them, gunning into reverse, the front left side of their sedan hitting a bit of curb, the fender lost in a cascade of sparks. Then they were out of the parking lot and gone.

Anton looked at Ivan.

"That did not go as expected," Ivan said.

The snow continued to fall.

Over the course of the next few hours, the scene only grew more surreal. At some point in the early afternoon, an entire squad of Moscow police arrived—but instead of confronting the balaclava-wearing strangers, they cordoned off the parking lot and a large section of the highway. Eventually, a fair number of journalists and photographers also arrived, gathering behind the police barricades, taking photos but not interfering.

It wasn't until after around five p.m. that things went from surreal to absolutely horrifying.

Three unmarked buses suddenly pulled past the barricades and entered the parking area. All three came to a stop next to the four unmarked cars—doors swinging open while the engines were still running. At least two dozen more men in balaclavas and flak jack-

41

ets poured out. Anton felt himself beginning to panic. Ivan had the shotgun up but still remained in his seat, shouting into the microphone in his coat.

The swarm of camouflaged men headed straight for the office building, submachine guns raised. There was a loud commotion, someone opening the glass doors from the inside. Anton watched as a handful of bodyguards rushed out, led by the head of security. The camouflaged men didn't even pause; a moment later, the head of security was facedown against the pavement. The other bodyguards had their hands in the air, facing the line of submachine guns.

Anton was about to shift his car into reverse, when there was a loud knock on the window to his left. He turned to see the barrel of one of the submachine guns touching the glass, inches from his face. The man outside in the balaclava said something, but his words were muffled. Even so, Anton had a fairly good idea what was expected.

Bulletproof glass or not, Anton didn't want to take any chances. He unlocked the door and allowed himself to be pulled from the car. The next thing he knew, he was facedown in the snow, a heavy boot on the back of his head. From his angle, he couldn't see much—but he could hear the voices of other men being dragged next to him, also pushed facedown into the frozen parking lot. For all he knew, his boss was right there with him, a boot against his tailored suit.

More than anything, that thought terrified him. You didn't take on a man like Vladimir Gusinsky in broad daylight—in front of half the journalists in Moscow—unless you were completely insane, or powerful enough to get away with it.

And for men with that much power, there wasn't much distance between making a man lie facedown in the snow . . . and putting a bullet in the back of his skull.

CHAPTER SIX

December 16, 1994,

Antigua, Caribbean

LEANING AGAINST THE WAIST-HIGH railing on the deck of a one-hundred-fifty-foot sailing yacht, staring out across an azure stretch of ocean, sun blasting the Moscow frost off his cheeks as the soft, salty breeze tugged at the corners of his open Armani shirt collar, Berezovsky began to understand why billionaires seemed obsessed with bigger and better boats.

Of course, there were boats, and then there were *boats*. The vessel beneath his feet was certainly impressive; comfortable, well--appointed cabins with room enough for five couples, a crew of at least sixteen, not including the bodyguards and the private chefs, parked in a secluded stretch of blue-on-blue water in the shadow of the exclusive playland island of Antigua. But it wasn't one of the true behemoths that would one day become synonymous with lifestyles of extreme wealth: the megayachts, with their multiple helipads, glass-bottomed swimming pools, lit-up disco floors, built-in pizza ovens, even submarines.

But Berezovsky wasn't going to quibble about which shade of

heaven he'd stepped into. The journey from Moscow to Antigua had been long and exhausting, and now that his bare feet were finally touching nautical wood, he could finally come as close to relaxing as his frenetic nature allowed.

Then he turned away from the water to face the deck behind him, taking in the small group of businessmen in shirts and shorts, the elegant, statuesque women in designer dresses from the highest-end stores in Paris, Milan, and even Moscow—and it seemed as though he hadn't traveled far at all. If it weren't the middle of December, and the temperature weren't kissing the mid-eighties, he might have thought he had just stepped into the well-heeled crowd on Tverskaya Street.

"Quite a juxtaposition," a soft voice chimed at him from his left, and he turned to see a young man—whom he knew, though not well—was now leaning back against the railing just a few feet away, legs crossed as he surveyed the scene. "Have to hand it to Pyotr for arranging this, it's much nicer than being stuck knee deep in a meter of snow."

Berezovsky smiled, taking in the man's sandy brown hair, two-day stubble, strong jaw, and piercing blue eyes. The man was around half his age, maybe mid-twenties, but he exuded the relaxed confidence of someone much older. He was wearing dark slacks and a white short-sleeved shirt with a polo player above his heart. He was pale, like Berezovsky, but had enough red in his cheeks to show that he had been in the Caribbean for a few days.

"It's easy to love the ocean," Berezovsky responded. "Pyotr has a very nice group of friends. And already I've seen a handful of fish—but only one or two whales."

The banking magnate Pyotr Aven, who had organized the junket and the boat, was certainly the latter. One of the wealthiest men in Russia, he was also one of the smartest. Like Berezovsky and Gusinsky, he had been born an outsider, but not impoverished, not underprivileged. And when the walls came down, he had parlayed the PhD in economics into a massive fortune.

The handsome young man next to Berezovsky was most decidedly still a fish, in Berezovsky's opinion, but maybe had the makings of a whale. Berezovsky knew Roman Abramovich as an entrepreneur from Moscow. They had had a little time to become reacquainted after landing in the island airport, and then again on the way to the yacht's tender.

Certainly, Abramovich had been quite familiar with Berezovsky and his accomplishments, even before they first met. Here on the boat, just as at the Presidential Club, Berezovsky drew everyone's attention. But among the group of businessmen gathered on the junket, the gazes weren't mocking, they were hungry. The purpose of this junket was business; more specifically, facilitating the sort of business relationships that turned fish into whales. And Berezovsky was rapidly becoming a man of consequence in this arena. Already, news of his impending privatization project involving ORT was swirling through the finance community. Added to his auto and banking interests, his interests in media gave him fingers in many, many pies.

The fish were hungry, because they knew that a man like Berezovsky, with his connections to the Family, could make things happen that were otherwise impossible. You could certainly become a millionaire in Russia without connections; Berezovsky himself had done so, and so had most of the men on the boat. But Berezovsky and the men who thought like him were no longer interested in making mere millions.

"I know it's early," Abramovich said, his voice as easy and confident as his posture, "but perhaps you have a moment for a proposition?"

And there it was, direct and without flourish. As Berezovsky had suspected, their meeting hadn't been the result of happenstance. Roman was in the Caribbean for a purpose, and Berezovsky was a potential means to an end. This thought didn't bother Berezovsky; quite the contrary, he enjoyed his position as a perceived power broker, and he loved nothing more than to be pursued. But with this young man, there was also something more.

A nice young man who probably has a commercial venture he wants to pitch me was how he'd first described Abramovich, when he'd called to check in with Badri Patarkatsishvili, his deputy director general at LogoVAZ and closest business partner. After a little checking up on Abramovich, he'd been impressed by the boyish entrepreneur's ambition, if not the moderate level of his success. Like the rest of them, Abramovich had started nowhere—truly, nowhere—orphaned by the age of four, his mother a victim of a blood disorder, his father killed in an accident at a construction site. He'd been shipped off to the Komi Republic to live with relatives—one of the harshest environments on the planet, a frozen tundra at the edge of the Arctic Circle where it was dark for more than three months out of the year. He'd studied engineering but had never graduated; after a stint in the army, he'd become a mechanic—but even at an early age, he'd seen himself as an entrepreneur.

"I can think of no better time or place," Berezovsky said. "But I hope your proposition doesn't involve rubber ducks."

Abramovich lost some of the color in his cheeks, until he saw that Berezovsky was joking. Indeed, the young man had begun his career running a toy company, manufacturing plastic playthings and, yes, rubber ducks. But soon after, he'd shifted into something much more lucrative: the trading and transportation of oil. How a high school dropout from the Arctic Circle with no connections could go from making rubber ducks to trading 3.5 million tons of petroleum products in just a few years was more than a little mysterious—but Berezovsky liked a little mystery. Compared to the circles Berezovsky frequented, Abramovich's trading company, though assuredly lucrative, was small-time. Still, he was intrigued by the man's youth and quick ascent. And then there was the lure of oil itself. There was money in cars, less so in TV—but oil was money in its true, liquid form.

And Berezovsky was certain Abramovich hadn't come to him seeking petroleum expertise.

"As you may know," Abramovich said, moving closer along the railing, "my trading company moves oil from the state refinery at Omsk in Siberia, which in turn gets its crude from the state-owned production units in Noyabrsk. I've spent the past few years familiarizing myself with this production line—from the drilling to the processing to the barrels I transport—and I've come to believe that, given the opportunity, I could do it better."

"By that you mean . . ."

"Vertically integrate, combine the production and refining businesses with my trading company. Run it along my already existing shipping network—and we've got an entire oil company moving petroleum across all of Europe."

Berezovsky no longer felt the boat rocking beneath his feet as he focused in on what the younger man was proposing. Berezovsky had been wrong when he had phoned Badri. This opportunity was much bigger than any simple commercial venture. Abramovich was talking about privatizing a massive, state-owned refinery and combining it with one of the largest producers of crude into one company. In a single swift act, they would be creating one of the world's largest oil businesses. Berezovsky felt his adrenaline rising at the thought.

"The business is one thing," he said, thinking aloud. "The politics quite another. But yes, this is perhaps something I could organize."

Abramovich fought a smile, but his eyes glittered like the Caribbean behind them.

"Of course the oil industry has its risks. It's a very competitive arena."

The young man didn't need to spell things out for Berezovsky; he was well aware of the industry's reputation. The same sorts who had shot up his car dealerships—and blown up his car—were endemic in the world of oil, and much fiercer. But, as Korzhakov had implied, Berezovsky was not the same man who had crawled out of that burning Mercedes. Berezovsky knew how to take care of the "competition."

Berezovsky found himself grinning as he thought of his rival, Gusinsky, and the scene that had been documented by dozens of journalists just two weeks ago. The spectacle had been so compelling, the press had even given it a name: Faces in the Snow. A dozen bodyguards dragged out into a parking lot, made to lie facedown in the snow for hours, while the Moscow police stood by impotently. Gusinsky himself had avoided arrest; but after Yeltsin's private security force had finally admitted they had conducted the raid—a "misunderstanding," they had explained, that had ended with a handful of Gusinsky's bodyguards in the hospital—the banking magnate had reportedly fled the country. He would be back, to be sure, but he had gotten the message. Berezovsky was not to be trifled with.

"Not a problem," he finally murmured, already thinking beyond the risks.

Oil—the potential was so vast, it was almost hard to calculate.

More intriguing, the company Abramovich was describing would create quite a regular stream of cash. And now that Berezovsky was on the verge of privatizing ORT, he was going to need access to a veritable river of rubles. ORT was losing money hand over fist; if he intended to make good on his promise to Korzhakov, to prop up Yeltsin as they headed into the next election cycle, he was going to need money to be coming in at an alarming rate.

"As long as we're being direct—how much profit does your trading company currently bring in?"

It wasn't exactly polite conversation, asking a man how much money he made. But there would be time for cocktail chatter later. For his part, Abramovich didn't seem put out by the question.

"Forty million a year."

"And if we can organize this proposal of yours—if we 'vertically integrate' Omsk and Noyabrskneftegaz—how much cash would you generate?"

"Maybe a hundred million a year?"

Berezovsky reached forward with both hands and clasped the younger man by the shoulders.

"It is from this that I will require certain funds to cover the expense of keeping things running smoothly."

Abramovich nodded, because he understood. Berezovsky didn't need to spell out what these expenses might be; he wasn't signing an employment contract, or even a partnership deal. Abramovich had come to him because of who he was—and what he brought to the table. His political connections, his protection, his roof. No doubt, Abramovich had done his research. He knew all about ORT, the Logovaz Club, and Berezovsky's lifestyle. He knew exactly what sort of deal they were about to strike.

Abramovich needed Berezovsky to privatize and combine the

refinery and petroleum production company into his trading business. And Berezovsky needed cash flow to keep ORT—and himself—afloat.

"Thirty million dollars per year, that should be a good place to start."

Research or no, Abramovich gaped at the number.

"That's almost my entire current trading profits."

"Correct, but when we organize this company, it will be an easy check to cash."

Abramovich swallowed, and thought it through. Berezovsky gave the young man his space, turning his attention back to the deck, where the small group of wealthy men and women were sharing war stories over cocktails served by the crew. He had no doubt that Abramovich would accept the deal. If there was one trait he could instantly recognize in others, it was ambition—and Abramovich, as mysterious as his past might be, had that familiar hunger in his soul. He didn't want to be a fish any longer, he didn't want to be sharing cocktails and trading stories on other men's boats. He wanted a giant boat of his own.

Which was why he finally nodded, then reached out once again, to shake Berezovksy's hand.

CHAPTER SEVEN

January 1995, afternoon,

Logovaz Club

I F THERE WAS EVER a face designed to capture the heart of a nation, Berezovsky thought to himself, as he settled into a leather love seat in a curtained alcove on the third floor of his private club, it belonged to the man sitting across from him.

"Thugs and gangsters," the man was saying, at the tail end of a monologue that had begun so long ago, Berezovsky had already finished two glasses of vodka in the interim, "and there is no place for either of them at ORT anymore."

Berezovsky nodded, as a waiter refilled his tumbler for the third time. The man sitting across from him—Vlad Listyev, easily the most popular television anchor in Russia—seemed to be struggling to contain his emotions, as his voice rose above the din of the moderately crowded drawing room. Berezovsky supposed his guest's animated demeanor was better than the stiff and awkward silence that had enveloped the man when he had first arrived at the Logovaz Club. Maybe it was the opulent setting that had initially caused his unease, or perhaps the newness of his own situation—he was, after all, a stranger to this world of business deals and handshake lunches. Or perhaps it was Berezovsky's Georgian business partner, seated not ten feet away on an antique daybed, pretending to read a newspaper. Badri Patarkatsishvili tended to have that effect on people. Even those who were blissfully unaware of his reputation.

Berezovsky had offered to move the meeting to his office on the top floor of the club, but thankfully, his guest had declined. The partially curtained alcove in the drawing room was private enough, and besides, what was the point of having such a famous face on his team if he was going to hide it behind an office door? You didn't hang a Picasso in the medicine cabinet, you stuck it right on the living room wall.

And what a famous face it was. Alive and glowing behind that bushy brown mustache, those square-framed glasses, that impressive, glossy hair. A face made for television, or more accurately, made *by* television.

Thirty-nine years old, in his trademark suspenders—supposedly modeled on the American television star Larry King—Listyev was perhaps the most famous man in the entire country. First as the host of his own talk show, which had a regular audience of over a hundred million people, and then as the beloved star of Russia's most popular game show, Vlad was a near daily presence in every Russian household. The hush that had moved through the Logovaz Club when Berezovsky had led him into the parlor had been palpable; even Badri had flushed behind his newspaper.

Choosing Vlad Listyev to run the newly privatized ORT had been an act of pure genius. Korzhakov had been right at the Presidential Club; the public would have had trouble envisioning a man like Berezovsky at the head of the nation's largest television network. But Vlad was a national treasure. He had the respect and experience necessary to run ORT, and a face that could easily help elect the president to his next term. No matter how much Yeltsin's health deteriorated, Berezovsky was convinced that ORT, with the help of Vlad Listyev, could prop him up through 1996.

Unfortunately, however, it was rapidly becoming apparent that there was more to Vlad Listyev than just his famous face.

"You disagree?" Vlad was half off his armchair, his eyes searing behind his square glasses. "This corruption, it's like a disease. These gangsters are like tumors, choking ORT from the inside."

"Your passion is inspiring," Berezovsky responded. "But we're not talking about life and death. These are television commercials."

Vlad's cheeks turned red as he shifted back into his seat.

"We're talking about more than commercials. We're talking about a system that is rotting at its core."

Vlad glanced past Berezovsky, toward an employee carrying a tray of exorbitantly expensive caviar. Berezovsky knew that Vlad was speaking about more than just ORT. Berezovsky did not doubt for a moment the anchorman's liberalism or his belief in President Yeltsin. He had been a voice for democracy from the very beginning. But he was also in a unique position to see the grime that was oiling the gears of this new capitalism.

Yet, despite his protestations, the grime in this situation really did have to do with television commercials. ORT wasn't losing a quarter of a billion dollars a year because people weren't watching. Vlad's own show had been getting ratings, which in America, would have been the equivalent of adding ABC, NBC, and CBS together. ORT was bleeding money because of a unique, very Russian advertising structure.

Instead of the network selling ads directly to independent companies, all ORT advertising was controlled by a single entity—a holding company made up of a consortium of shareholders. This arrangement had led to an incredible amount of graft—of which Berezovsky was intimately aware, since LogoVAZ was, in fact, one of the minor shareholders in the consortium. Though he agreed with Vlad's assessment—that the advertising structure was utterly corrupt—he admired the creativity behind it, though he couldn't take credit for its invention. That honor fell to a young, reportedly well-connected businessman who had built his wealth running disco clubs and dance halls.

"It's a complex business," Berezovsky started.

"There's a difference between businessmen and gangsters."

"Yes," Berezovsky said. "Usually it's the size of their wallet."

That got a grunt from Badri on the other side of the alcove.

Vlad brought a hand down against his knee, then removed his glasses and lowered his voice.

"It's time to change things. And I think I know how we should do this. I'm going to enact a moratorium on all advertising for the next few months. For the time being, ORT will sell no ads until this corruption is shaken out."

Berezovsky heard Badri's newspaper ruffle. Berezovsky cleared his throat.

"There are often better ways to treat a tumor than immediately reaching for a knife."

"We don't need to treat the tumor. We need to take it out."

Berezovsky looked at the famous man. A moratorium on advertising was going to cost a lot of people an enormous amount of money. He began to calculate, thinking forward through the possible outcomes of such a maneuver. Who was going to lose and who was going to gain. What mattered most, of course, was where he landed on that spectrum. Initially, he would certainly lose; but as a major part of ORT, if Vlad could somehow right the ship— it could make things very interesting.

"Perhaps a drink as we think this through," Berezovsky said, but Vlad cut him off, rising from his seat.

"None for me, thank you."

"Of course."

Berezovsky had read that the man had recently beaten his alcoholism—one of the many obstacles the man had overcome. Vlad's biography read like something out of a Dostoyevsky novel: a father who had committed suicide when he was young, a mother who drank, two children who had died young.

What could Berezovsky teach a man like that?

It wasn't until Vlad had entered the elevator leading down to the security driveway, the twin steel doors closing shut behind him, that Badri lowered his newspaper and glanced at Berezovsky. As usual, the Georgian's expression was hard to read. His eyes were bright and amiable, but most of his features were hidden behind his handlebar mustache, which he twisted between the fingers of his left hand.

"It's not going to go over well. This moratorium."

"You think he will be a problem?" Berezovsky asked.

"The dance hall king? Of course. He's always a problem."

"Not him."

Vlad's floral cologne still hung in the air. He was a legend, beloved by everyone. He was also very smart.

"He's a good man. He loves his country almost as much as we love him. He wants things to be better."

Berezovsky nodded, still thinking.

"And the dance hall king? You can talk to him?"

It was what Badri did. He had been one of the heads of Logo-VAZ since the beginning, and now he was an official with ORT—

but his real job, his real skill, was communication. Specifically, he could communicate with the type of people Vlad was trying to chase out of television.

"It's going to cost us a lot of money," Badri said.

Berezovsky grunted. In the short term. ORT in general was going to cost a lot of money, but, as he'd told Korzhakov, that wasn't the point. His thoughts immediately turned to the young man on the Caribbean yacht. Roman Abramovich's integrated oil company—and his payment of thirty million dollars a year—would be just the beginning. The possibilities were endless. Oil to prop up television to prop up a president who would prop up Berezovsky.

Round and round and round it went.

Which brought him back to Vlad Listyev. Did Berezovsky need to reassess his previous opinions? Had choosing the anchorman to run ORT been a stroke of genius, or a mistake? Vlad was a good man—a truly good man. Did that make him a liability?

For once, Berezovsky wasn't sure.

CHAPTER EIGHT

March 1, 1995, 8:55 p.m.,

Novokuznetskaya Street, Moscow

IT WAS THE MOST incredible feeling in the world.

The warmth of the bright spots trained on his makeup-caked face, the hush in the studio as the producer counted down the seconds, the soft breeze from the boom mike lowering above his head. And then that frantic burst of adrenaline, as the camera blinked on, capturing the particles of light reflecting off his face, translating his visage into electronic packets, streaming him through cables and off satellite dishes and into wire antennas all over his beloved country, multiplying him a hundred million times, delivering him into living rooms and kitchens and appliance stores on every block in every city across the greatest nation in the world. His essence, everywhere, for everyone—because that's really all anyone was, after all—light reflected off skin and clothes and bones.

Vlad Listyev was not a religious man. Hell, with a background like his it was impossible to believe in much beyond some twisted game of fate—but when that camera flashed on, he felt connected to the world in a way that truly hinted at a higher power. Even now, walking home from the evening broadcast of his signature show, *Chas Pik*, the cold night air biting at his skin, he could still feel that energy pulsing through him. The pretty, tree-lined street near the heart of Moscow was quiet, save for the odd car rumbling past, and the sound of the breeze riffling through the nearly bare tree branches above his head. But in his mind, one hundred million voices pushed him on. They were listening, they were watching. *They were always watching.*

Vlad's pace quickened as he caught sight of his apartment building, just a dozen yards ahead. The first day of March in Moscow was often indistinguishable from the heart of winter—but tonight, it felt much more like the first day of spring. A moment of rebirth and change.

Most of Vlad's closest friends thought that perhaps he had gone completely crazy. Accepting the position as the head of the newly privatized ORT, dipping his toes into the business world at a time like this—the water so infested that it was impossible to tell the sharks from the fish—certainly seemed to have the color of madness.

What his friends did not understand—it was his love for his people that pushed him to make this decision. He wasn't a businessman, but he didn't see ORT as a business.

He pulled his overcoat tighter against his throat as he reached the entrance to his apartment building. A man like Berezovsky might never be able to understand, but Vlad's plan to chase the corruption out of television by imposing a moratorium on ads wasn't a business strategy. He didn't want to clean up ORT to make Berezovsky richer. He saw television as something much, much bigger than a corporation. Just as the cameras captured his reflection, spinning it a hundred million times across the country, those same cameras reflected something back—a picture of what his nation had become. So much promise, so much possibility, but tethered to a corrupt time.

Almost out of instinct, Vlad glanced behind himself at the empty sidewalk, taking note of the few cars on the street beside him. He knew that it was a risky game he was playing. The corrupt forces aligned against him were not going to look kindly on his moratorium or the tens of millions of dollars they would lose because of it. But Vlad was optimistic. He believed that eventually, they would find other businesses to conquer—or they would simply accept what he was trying to do. The idea that he might come to physical harm over television ads seemed incredibly unlikely.

Even so, he wasn't a fool. In fact, just a day ago, he had been visited by a pair of government agents who had told him that although there weren't any specific threats against him, he needed to be careful. But, despite his wife's insistence, he wasn't going to lock himself up like an Oligarch, with bodyguards and armored cars. Despite the corruption of the moment, despite what he read in the newspapers every day and reported on his television shows, he believed in his people.

Perhaps that was part of the Russian condition, to love something so broken and bruised. Perhaps it was the same reason his people had embraced him—a man who at times had been so broken and bruised. Hell, if he couldn't take a stand, then who could?

He took the steps up to the doorway to his apartment building, undid the dead bolt, and stepped inside.

To his surprise, the foyer was darker than usual; he noticed that one of the bulbs in the stairwell leading up into the interior of the building had blown out—but there was still just enough light to make out the steps.

He was halfway to the first landing when he realized that he hadn't heard the front door shut behind him. He was about to turn to see why—when he noticed movement a few feet above him.

He squinted through his glasses—and made out a man, dressed entirely in black, his face covered by what appeared to be a ski mask.

Vlad froze midstep. His mind started to try to make sense of what he was seeing, and he reached down toward his coat. He had a fair amount of cash on him, and the rational portion of his brain thought maybe this was a robbery.

And then he heard the two sudden pops. Something bit at his arm, right above the elbow, and then something else touched the back of his head. Suddenly he was falling, the muscles in his legs giving out. A warm river was running down the back of his neck—but his mind was already beginning to disconnect as he toppled down the stairs.

Before his eyes stopped working, he caught a glimpse of one of the men standing in the open doorway behind him, also dressed in black. In the man's hand was a 9mm handgun, attached to a cruel-looking silencer.

Perhaps Vlad's final sense, his final emotion, was pure disbelief; that even in this new and brutal Russia, a man could be murdered over television commercials.

And then his body hit the ground.

CHAPTER NINE

March 2, 1995, 3:00 p.m.,

Logovaz Club

IN MOMENTS LIKE THESE—JUST the two of them, alone in Berezovsky's private office on the top floor of the club, the slight businessman hunched over his desk, Litvinenko standing a few feet away, his hip against an ornate window sill as he watched the Oligarch work—Litvinenko could almost forget the gulf between them, the marathon of education, wealth, and political status that would forever mark them as employer and employee. He could almost forget that he was little more than a glorified cop, moonlighting for a few extra dollars and perhaps a chance at something more, while Berezovsky was a man with hundreds of millions in the bank, who had, on at least two occasions that Litvinenko knew of, dined with the president. Marina, Litvinenko's ballroom dancer, liked to joke that Litvinenko was a member of the chorus brushing elbows with one of the principal players, whenever he made his weekly visit to the Logovaz, but Litvinenko liked to believe that the relationship had progressed a bit beyond that.

In fact, in his mind, in less than a year, he and the Oligarch had developed something that could almost be called a friendship. At first, Berezovsky had been understandably wary of the FSB agent. Even though Litvinenko had been an officer investigating the assassination attempt on Berezovsky's life, the businessman had not expected more than a few cursory Q-and-A sessions, maybe a couple of arrests that would eventually lead nowhere. He had been surprised by Litvinenko's apparent dedication to unraveling the details of the bombing. Although the FSB had eventually run into dead ends, Litvinenko had managed to impress Berezovsky with his willingness to turn over as many rocks as he could, and more significantly, with his sincerity and compassion.

Eventually, Berezovsky had begun to invite him to meet on a more regular basis to discuss things even beyond the assassination attempt. They had discovered many similar beliefs and predilections; Litvinenko had told him all about his ballroom dancer, how he had fallen in love with her the first time he'd seen her dance, vowing that she would one day be his wife. Berezovsky seemed to have a blonde for every day of the week, but he understood the importance of passion, and his love for all things beautiful informed most aspects of his daily life.

Surprisingly, the two men also held many similar political opinions, and they shared a growing dislike of the war in Chechnya. For his part, Berezovsky was against the war because it wasn't particularly good for business. Litvinenko had served in the Chechen expansion, had seen the violence up close. He'd been waist high in the mud of that war, but, as he'd told Marina when he'd finally made his way home, he'd done all he could to still be able to hold her with clean hands.

Litvinenko couldn't pinpoint the exact moment when his and Berezovsky's association had shifted enough to the point where the

Oligarch felt comfortable trusting the FSB agent with some of his business needs, but sometime in the past six months, Litvinenko had found himself on the businessman's payroll. Although he had once looked down upon his colleagues who had taken moonlighting jobs, after he had begun enjoying the fruits of employment outside the leaky government bureaucracy, he had found the steady addition to his income quite seductive. Berezovsky's demands so far hadn't been extreme; a background check here, a phone record there. He'd still been able to come home to Marina each night with clean hands.

Usually, when they met here in Berezovsky's office, the conversation remained light and airy. This particular early evening session had been quieter than usual; the event of the previous day infused every passing thought. Even if Alexander hadn't been an FSB agent who specialized in counterterrorism and acts of crime, and Berezovsky a businessman personally connected to the tragedy, the sense of mourning in the air would have been just as palpable.

The death of Vlad Listyev had struck Russia like a sledgehammer. As the details of his assassination emerged, the entire nation was gripped by a sense of horror and sadness, followed by anger. That something like this could happen to such a man so beloved—it was truly unthinkable. The day after the murder, walking through the streets of Moscow on his way to Berezovsky's office, Litvinenko had passed groups of people dressed in black, huddled in deep and sorrowful discussion. Pictures in the newspaper had shown throngs of shocked and sobbing fans of the journalist lining the barricades in front of Listyev's apartment building, where the crime had taken place. President Yeltsin himself had declared a day of mourning, and all the television stations had gone dark. ORT had replaced its regular programming with a single photo of the anchorman, captioned by the simple statement *Vlad Listyev has been killed.*

The press conference Yeltsin had called had been much less sedate. Yeltsin himself had made an appearance, and had opened the event with a fiery, podium-pounding statement, taking full responsibility for an act that seemed to mark a true change in the barbarism that had taken over the streets of the new Russia: "I bow my head, as a man who has not done enough to fight banditry, corruption, bribery, and crime."

Litvinenko had seen his fair share of atrocities—murders, bombings, mutilations—but this was clearly a watershed.

One didn't need to be an FSB agent to see that Vlad's death was a professional assassination and not a robbery gone bad. Listyev had been shot twice from behind, once in the arm and once in the back of the head. His assailants had not relieved him of more than $1,500 in American currency—and the million-plus rubles—that he'd been carrying in his overcoat.

Litvinenko had no idea who had murdered the most famous man in Russia. He was not involved in the investigation, and he only knew what he had read in the newspaper—that the journalist had recently been put in charge of ORT by Berezovsky and his business partners, that he was determined to root out corruption in the television business. That information alone told Litvinenko there would be a long list of potential suspects. He had no doubt that the tense and somber moment he and his boss were having was being replayed everywhere, in kitchens, dining rooms, and living rooms all across the country. A single murder, and it felt like the ground had shifted.

Even so, Litvinenko was not mentally prepared when the door to Berezovsky's office was suddenly flung inward, and two policemen stepped inside, pushing their way past a pair of the Oligarch's bodyguards. Both men were wearing uniforms from the local Moscow directorate, and both had holstered sidearms. The lead officer was heavyset, his second thin and tall, and both were entirely focused on the businessman behind the desk. If they even noticed Litvinenko's presence, they didn't acknowledge him.

"Boris Berezovsky," shouted the lead officer. "Please stand up. We have orders to bring you in for questioning, on the matter of the murder of Vlad Listyev."

Litvinenko felt his stomach knot. He had no idea who had sent these men to Berezovsky's office, or how they had worked their way through the Logovaz Club without being stopped by the phalanx of bodyguards inside. Nor did he know anything about the ongoing investigation into the anchorman's assassination—whether there were any real suspects, whether any arrests had already been made.

Litvinenko did know that the two policemen in front of him were cogs, not levers. Their uniforms meant they had come for Berezovsky at somebody else's order. If they left this office with Berezovsky in tow, there was a good chance Litvinenko was going to be out of a job.

He didn't have time to think; in a split-second decision, he took a step out from behind the desk, squaring his shoulders as he faced the two officers. The men shifted their attention to him from Berezovsky, their faces puzzled. They had no reason to recognize him. Although he had taken part in a number of investigations into terrorist-related incidents in the city, his position with the FSB did not place him in direct contact with the local police very often. But his demeanor certainly communicated to the two policemen that he wasn't intimidated by their uniforms.

"I believe there's been a mistake."

The lead officer turned back to Berezovsky, a hand resting on his holstered automatic.

"Boris Berezovsky," he repeated. "We have orders to take you in."

Litvinenko could see the red splotches rising in Berezovsky's cheeks. If Litvinenko didn't do something quickly, this was going to escalate.

"If you have a warrant for Mr. Berezovsky's arrest, please hand it over."

The officer looked back at Litvinenko, whose fingers tightened against his weapon. Litvinenko was now certain: there was no warrant, there were no arrest orders. The Moscow Police was a fiefdom.

Litvinenko made another decision—and slowly unhooked the clasps of his holster, partially drawing his gun, his fingers loose against the grip.

"You have no right to take this man anywhere."

The two policemen stared at him in shock. The air in the room became tight as a coiled snake.

Then the lead officer's hand seemed to loosen against his own holster.

"Who are you?"

"My name is Alexander Litvinenko. I'm an FSB officer, and I am one hundred percent certain that Mr. Berezovsky was not involved in this tragic murder."

With his other hand, Litvinenko retrieved his official papers from his shirt pocket and offered them to the policemen. He kept his gun loose, as the lead officer inspected the documents.

"We have our orders," the second officer tried again, lamely.

"Yes, we all have our orders," Litvinenko responded. "Mr. Berezovsky is an innocent man under the protection of the FSB. If you would like to take it up with my superiors, feel free to make an appointment."

Another moment passed in silence—and then the two police officers turned and walked out of the room. It wasn't until their footsteps had receded that Litvinenko felt his chest relax and noticed the rivulets of sweat running down the back of his neck. FSB, Moscow Police, Oligarchs, Politicians: in a moment like the one that had just transpired, none of the labels really mattered. What mattered was that a gun, even partially drawn, always trumped a gun in a holster.

Berezovsky whistled low, and then came up out of his seat. He beckoned Litvinenko over—and then embraced him in a warm hug.

Then he reached for the phone on his desk.

"To accuse me of this tragedy, it is unthinkable."

He looked at Litvinenko as he dialed the Kremlin.

"You have shown me something today I will not forget."

Litvinenko's fingers shook as he resecured his gun.

Before tonight, he had a job. Now he had a krysha.

CHAPTER TEN

January 1996,

Logovaz Club

MARINA GONCHAROVA HAD ALWAYS considered herself an extremely practical woman. It was perhaps the main reason she had become an accountant in the first place; there was something wonderfully reassuring about numbers corralled into equations, and systems that functioned along logical and mathematical frameworks. That didn't mean she had an aversion to creative thinking; being an accountant in modern Russia necessitated a certain amount of *creativity*. But nothing in her half decade as one of Roman Abramovich's most trusted number crunchers could have prepared her for the utterly surreal moment that was now unfolding in front of her.

Which was probably why she quickly decided to approach the situation in a very narrow, *practical* way: a one-hundred-five-pound woman in a pantsuit, long blond hair tied up in a bun, hauling a forty-three pound suitcase up a flight of stairs.

Just getting the damn thing from the armored car parked out front, through the back security entrance of the Logovaz Club, had taken the help of two of the bodyguards her employers had sent with her from Abramovich's offices. Unfortunately, the Logovaz's own security team hadn't been keen on letting her men escort her into the building. So here she was now, on her own, dragging what felt like a ship's anchor wrapped in polyester, step by torturous step. The Logovaz security men now standing by, gawking at her, had offered to help—one of them had even made a grab for the suitcase—but Marina had slapped his hand away. She didn't know these men, and the last thing she was going to do was let someone else handle the package she had been sent to deliver.

She did her best to tune out the men watching her, as she focused on her efforts, the muscles in her forearms and thighs straining against the expensive material of her suit. She had taken only a few steps before her progress was suddenly interrupted by a young man with slicked-back hair and a tailored blue jacket rushing down from the top of the steps and skidding to a stop in front of her.

"Excuse me, miss. Can I help you?" he asked, his voice nearly cracking.

Marina didn't know the young man by sight, but she was pretty sure his name was Ivan. She had been told that one of Berezovsky's assistants would meet her at the door—and yet, even so, she wasn't about to hand off the heavy suitcase to this kid whom she'd never met before.

"I have a package that I need to pass on to Mr. Berezovsky," she said, "And as you can see, it's rather large. So it's going to take me some time."

Ivan held out a thin, pale hand.

"You can leave it with me."

Marina shook her head, her bun bouncing with the motion.

"No. I have to transfer this package myself. I have to pass this on personally, namely to Mr. Berezovsky."

Ivan didn't seem pleased at all—but Marina didn't really care. She was an accountant, this man was an assistant—and the contents of the suitcase were well beyond both their responsibility levels. Marina knew this for certain, because she had packed the damn thing herself. *And that, alone, had been an experience she was certain she would never forget.*

There was a frozen, awkward moment, while Ivan tried to figure out what to do and continued to block her progress up the stairs. Finally he shrugged and guided her forward toward the lobby of the club. At least one of the nearby security men snickered at the sight of the slight young woman towing a heavy suitcase—while the impotent assistant simply led the way—but Marina ignored him. She knew they were all bit players in this farce, witnesses who saw nothing that their employers didn't want them to see, who heard nothing but what they were told to hear.

Even so, it was hard for Marina not to feel self-conscious, as they slowly worked their way through the various floors of the Logovaz. She had never been in this place before and felt out of place in the crowded club, especially around the expensive suits of the businessmen and designer cocktail dresses of their guests. Marina couldn't help but wonder if Ivan found the moment as surreal as she did; then again, working for a man like Berezovsky, he had probably seen many things even more bizarre than an accountant pulling a heavy suitcase.

The truth was, moments like these were part of the new way of doing business in Russia, although this instance was an extreme. As a trusted employee of Roman Abramovich for many years now—and in her new position, at the "formation in process" of Sibneft—she had already experienced her share of surreal events.

History would one day judge the goings on of the preceding

weeks. A combination of applied genius, force of will, and the ability to navigate through a corrupt system—all perfectly executed by two men. While they brought very different skill sets, they had managed to create one of the largest oil companies in history almost out of thin air.

They say that in business everything is timing, and in this case, the timing could not have been more perfect; Abramovich, with his idea of combining the two state-owned businesses—the oil refinery in Omsk and the production company in Noyabrsk—had caught Berezovsky at exactly the right moment; falling directly in the midst of his privatization of ORT, in an effort to advance the candidacy of Yeltsin in the upcoming election.

The months that had followed the Caribbean cruise had only inflated Berezovsky's position and the potential of his ORT proposal—as Yeltsin's own status had grown more precarious. The president was facing a real threat in the Communist candidate Gennady Zyuganov—while Yeltsin's health had begun to deteriorate at an even faster pace. There were always rumors of heart issues, even impending surgery. Without ORT and Berezovsky's promise to use the network as a publicity tool, Yeltsin might lose the presidency. And if the Communists took over, it would be a disaster for the business community.

After the cruise, it had been relatively easy for Berezovsky to convince his contacts in the Yeltsin government that for ORT to continue its operations and campaign for Yeltsin, the network would need a massive and sudden infusion of money—especially after the freezing of advertising that Vlad Listyev had enacted right before his untimely death. Like Yeltsin, ORT was in a precarious state.

Privatizing an oil company would essentially give ORT—and Yeltsin's campaign—a bottomless war chest. Once the concept had been accepted, it had just become a matter of putting the pieces in place. The first step: Abramovich and Berezovsky had needed to convince the Red Directors who ran the state-owned refinery and the production plant to agree to the unification of the company—under new management.

Since Abramovich had previously established relationships with the Red Directors—Viktor Gorodilov in Noyabrsk, and Ivan Litskevich at the refinery in Omsk—from his years in oil trading, he began the process of convincing the two men that he could indeed run the company in a way that would benefit them all. Eventually, Berezovsky had joined in on the efforts, using his status to further push the directors in the right direction.

Gorodilov had acquiesced fairly easily, but Litskevich had resisted; at one point he seemed to be becoming a true roadblock to the endeavor. Concerned, Berezovsky had written a personal letter to the director, asking him to trust Roman Abramovich as he obviously did himself. Thankfully, the letter had been unnecessary, and Berezovsky's status and political capital hadn't been needed to convince the man to change his mind. In the sort of coincidence of timing that seemed to happen more and more often in modern Russia, at some point during the weeks the merger was being discussed, Litskevich had organized a late-night party for himself and an attractive young woman on the banks of the Irtysh River; halfway into the tryst, Litskevich decided to try to impress his date by jumping into the frozen waters in front of them—and almost instantly after hitting the 7-degree water, had a heart attack and drowned. His driver—one of the few witnesses to the event—died in a bar fight shortly afterward.

Thankfully, Litskevich's replacement had been more acquiescent, and soon both Red Directors were ready to play ball. The pieces for privatization were in place.

The privatization system had been honed through practice in the short time since Berezovsky had fought his way to a stake in ORT, beginning in late fall of 1994. Since then, through 1995 and into 1996, the Russian government, desperate for funds to shore up its abysmal financial situation, had embarked on what was commonly known as a "loans for shares" program. Simply put, shares of state owned conglomerates were offered as collateral for "loans" that were in turn auctioned off for cash, usually to privately held banks. When the state defaulted on these loans—which, from the very beginning, it fully intended to do—the bank either became the owner of the shares, or sold them in a prearranged transaction to a new private owner.

These "loans for shares" auctions had already transferred some of the country's largest companies into the hands of a few lucky souls. The largest nickel manufacturer in Russia had been traded for 170 million dollars—and was now a private company that would soon be worth more than one billion dollars. Mikhael Khodorkovsky, a brilliant young physicist who had gone into banking, among other things, had achieved a nearly eighty percent controlling stake in Yukos, one of the country's largest oil companies, for around 350 million dollars—a deal that would soon make him the richest man in Russia and, indeed, one of the richest men in the world. There was no telling what Yukos would eventually be worth.

At first glance, to an accountant such as Marina—a woman who understood the new Russia and what it was faced with—selling off state resources to men with money was a desperate, but not intrinsically corrupt effort. Western buyers had no interest in dealing with Russia; they found the market too dangerous. The government was nearly broke, and without a cash infusion, there was a real chance it would go belly up. Anatoly Chubais, who had spearheaded the privatization program in the first place, believed that the quicker the state sold off companies to private owners, the less likely the

Communists could undo the progress they were making. He firmly believed that each sale was like a nail in communism's coffin. "We must sell it all," he had said on various occasions—believing that if they sold enough assets, the situation would be irreversible.

And the auctions themselves seemed fair on the surface—but Marina understood this wasn't truly the case. The transition to capitalism had left her country running under a system of patronage, krysha, and graft; it was not going to become an egalitarian market overnight. The auctions that decided the outcomes of the "loans for shares" offers were usually locked up beforehand.

The auction that resulted in the right to manage Sibneft was no different, and it took significant behind-the-scenes maneuvering to make sure that Abramovich and Berezovsky had been the only real bidders for a controlling situation in the newly formed oil company. As the final days approached, there had still been two other interested parties; Berezovsky sent his business partner, Badri Patarkatsishvili, the Georgian, to speak with them, and the situation was all stitched up in short order. Though Abramovich carried two bids in his pocket to the auction—one much higher than he could actually afford—he was able to win right around the initial offering, for 110 million dollars.

The only problem that remained was that Abramovich didn't have anywhere near that kind of money; to that end, he had been able to convince one of his colleagues—an Oligarch by the name of Alexander Smolenski, who ran one of the larger banks in Moscow—to provide credit for the purchase—which was repaid using money from the newly formed Sibneft. In all, Abramovich had put up around seventeen million dollars of his own money—and gained control of one of the largest oil companies in Russia.

A surreal series of events that had led Marina to this even more surreal moment. She often wondered what future economists would make of the "loans for shares" initiative—would they take into account the context, the sudden transfer from one form of market to another? A setting in which the rule of law was effectively turned on its head, where the government was locked in a desperate battle for survival, where corruption ran rampant in the quest to quickly relocate a massive amount of wealth and resources? In fact, the pairing of Abramovich and Berezovsky—the young, brilliant, creative entrepreneur and the connected power broker with fingers in the Kremlin—was uniquely designed for this context.

Marina's boss had calculated correctly when he had chosen Berezovsky to help him create Sibneft; but, of course, there was a price to be paid—and somehow Marina had found herself in the middle. She was essentially a pencil pusher—who was now pushing a heavy suitcase across the top floor of the Logovaz Club, right up to the entrance to Boris Berezovsky's office.

Once again, Ivan tried to step in front and stop her as she reached the partially open door. The two bodyguards who were stationed outside the door were about to help with his efforts—but Marina didn't give them the chance. She quickly pushed between them, yanking the suitcase after her.

She had never met Boris Berezovsky before—she wasn't even certain what he looked like—but she could easily tell that the diminutive man at the desk on the other side of the lavish office, speaking quickly and in clipped tones into a telephone—wasn't used to being interrupted. Ivan quickly came around her, obsequiously using his hands to apologize to his boss for the intrusion—an action that only seemed to make Berezovsky angrier. As soon as the Oligarch had finished with the phone conversation, he hurled the phone at Ivan, striking the young man in the chest.

Marina's face blanched—and she realized that this was a good cue to make her exit. She quickly pushed the suitcase a few more feet into the office, then turned and hurried back the way she had come. The bodyguards watched her go—and she could clearly hear the door to the office shut behind her.

She wondered what sort of reaction Berezovsky would exhibit when he eventually opened the suitcase. She had to imagine that even a man of his means would be affected by the sight of one million dollars in American currency. Marina herself had never seen anything like it—had never thought she would see that kind of money in one place. When the people from the bank had brought the banded stacks of cash to Abramovich's offices, Marina had spent a good ten minutes just looking at the piles of bills before she had begun to pack them into the suitcase.

From everything she had been told about Boris Berezovsky, she doubted he would take anywhere near that long before he dug his hands into his first krysha payment. Marina was equally certain, as she worked her way back down through the extravagant Logovaz Club, that this surreal moment was likely to be just the first of many.

The contents of the suitcase might represent a monstrous sum to a woman like Marina, but a million dollars wasn't going to satisfy a man like Boris Berezovsky for very long.

CHAPTER ELEVEN

February 1996,

World Economic Forum, Annual Meeting,

Davos, Switzerland

T WO MONTHS BEFORE HIS fiftieth birthday, and Boris Berezovsky could count on the fingers of one hand the number of times he had been rendered speechless—and one of those times had involved a blown-up Mercedes and a decapitated driver. But here it was, happening again in the most pristine setting he could ever imagine: an elegant, wood-paneled conference room in an alpine hotel, hanging off the edge of the most spectacular, snow-topped mountain, the air outside so crisp and blue it was like the frozen interior of a diamond. It was a place that had been chosen—if not designed—for the coming together of the brilliant and the powerful, a place created for conversation, for a quest for common ground. And yet here Berezovsky sat, anchored to his chair, suddenly shocked into silence.

He was alone in the rectangular room, his back to an oversize fireplace that sent concentric waves of fragrant heat through the material of his tailored suit. The man with whom he had been meeting for the past hour had excused himself at least ten minutes before—

but still Berezovsky hadn't moved, his mind reviewing the conversation he had just endured.

He knew that the gist of what had been said was nothing he shouldn't have already known; he had been having similar conversations for the past ten days in Moscow, and the man who had just left the Alpine conference room hadn't said anything Berezovsky could not have realized himself. But hearing those words, in this place, from such a source—it was beyond sobering.

George Soros, the Hungarian-born American billionaire, one of the richest men in the world—and in many ways a personal idol of Berezovsky's—was exactly the sort of man you came to the World Economic Forum at Davos to meet. To Berezovsky, he represented everything laudable about the West; Soros's opinions informed Berezovsky of the Western way of thinking about markets, business, and even politics. Berezovsky had searched him out specifically to get his opinion on the situation that was rapidly developing back in his homeland.

There was now no doubt—the political situation had gotten to be well beyond desperate. Though Berezovsky's personal status had continued to rise—both with his success with ORT and his assistance in privatizing Sibneft—his optimism about the upcoming election and Yeltsin's chances of staying president had begun to fray. The Yeltsin government was moments away from complete catastrophe. Yeltsin himself had physically deteriorated, his worsening health preventing all but a few public appearances in the past few weeks. Meanwhile, the Communists had resurged, winning a majority in the State Duma in a recent surprise election—and they had brought forth a remarkably popular candidate to run against Yeltsin—Gennady Zyuganov. At the moment, Zyuganov had a resounding lead over Yeltsin in every poll; Yeltsin was sitting at a mere three percent approval rating, the lowest of his career, perhaps a reaction to the perception that his government was corrupt, perhaps just a sign that people were terrified that his government might fail.

Still, coming to Davos, the central, most significant gathering of the international elite, where business and political leaders from all over the world came together to speak about the present and the future—Berezovsky had had reason to believe that all was not lost. He and the handful of Russian Oligarchs and politicians who had traveled to Switzerland with him—including members of Yeltsin's "Family," a group now spearheaded by Anatoly Chubais—had assumed that the Western leaders and businessmen would rally around Yeltsin. After all, the president was the only true democratic prospect in Russia, a capitalist who was trying his best to bring Russia into the modern era.

Instead, when Berezovsky and his colleagues had arrived in Switzerland, they had witnessed the unthinkable: the Western leaders had fallen all over themselves in an attempt to get close to Zyuganov and the Communists. It was almost as though the rest of the world was endorsing a fall backward to the Soviet era. Berezovsky knew the endorsements Zyuganov was getting had more to do with pure opportunism—he was the front-runner, and if the West wanted to do business in Russia, they needed the support of whoever became president—but even so, he had expected the West to stand behind democracy and capitalism, whatever the risk.

So he had arranged the meeting with George Soros, the businessman for whom he had more respect than any other. He had been seeking advice, perhaps a road map to get Yeltsin back on track.

Berezovsky didn't remember every word that the Western businessman had spoken, but his most vivid remarks on the situation seemed still to be twirling through the high-altitude, oxygen-depleted air: *You should think about leaving Russia, Boris. You are not just going to lose this election—you are going to end up hanging from a lamppost.*

Soros had gotten one thing correct. This was an existential battle; a Communist president wouldn't just roll back the capitalistic changes of the past decade—a shift to communism would mean the end of the line for Berezovsky and his colleagues. Privatization? Gone. Sibneft, Yukos, ORT, all of it would end up back in the hands of the state, and people like Berezovsky and Abramovich might find themselves in prison—or worse.

Berezovsky felt his pulse quicken, a sudden fire rising in his veins. The last time he had experienced sensations like this had also been in Switzerland—while he recuperated from the burns covering his arms and face. He was not a man who stopped fighting unless there was no other option, and despite what George Soros and the Western bankers and politicians at Davos might be thinking, he refused to accept that this battle was over.

But he also knew it wasn't a battle he could fight alone. Which meant that he needed to make amends and befriend the very people he was in constant competition with—the other men who had benefited from the Yeltsin era, men who had just as much to lose.

Regardless of what Berezovsky had told Korzhakov, ORT alone—even financed heavily by Sibneft—wasn't going to be enough to turn the public over to Yeltsin. One television station, even as enormous as ORT, could reach only a certain segment of the population, and it was already well known to be leaning heavily in Yeltsin's favor. Berezovsky needed more weapons in his arsenal: media, and also money, more than he alone could ever organize. The coffers of one of the biggest oil companies in Russia were one thing—but what about the coffers of *all* the oil companies, *and* the nickel companies, *and* the aluminum companies? What about the coffers of all the recently privatized resources of one of the wealthiest nations on the planet?

The idea grew inside of him. The press liked to call them Oligarchs, and most of Berezovsky's colleagues bristled at the name. But that's exactly what Berezovsky now had in mind, a group of Oligarchs who would turn the election on its head. Not only because it was in their best interests, but because it was in the best interests of the country, and the only real road to democracy. A happy coincidence, perhaps, but one that Berezovsky could hold aloft like a torch. *He wasn't looting Russia, he was saving it.*

This would mean making friends with former enemies—specifically, men like Vladimir Gusinsky, the owner of NTV and the man he'd nearly had run out of the country for good. And it would also mean confronting former friends—as enemies. Hard-liners in Yeltsin's government—a handful in the "Family"—were making a loud racket, pushing forward proposals to hold onto power no matter how the election went. Conservatives, former military men such as Korzhakov, as well as the current prime minister and a number of others in the cabinet, intended to keep Yeltsin in office using an old-school methodology—simply postponing an election that he couldn't win.

In contrast, Berezovsky found himself on the side of democracy, along with Yeltsin's daughter Tatiana and Anatoly Chubais, his brilliant strategist. The battle between the two sides had been growing more terrifying each day, as the election drew near, and there were even brewing fears of a real coup.

Berezovsky wouldn't have put anything past Korzhakov. But Berezovsky also believed that if push came to shove, Yeltsin's favor would swing toward his beloved daughter over his drinking buddy (and sometimes right-hand man and longtime head of security). Still, binding together the Oligarchs—financiers whom Korzhakov disliked, as a group—in support of democracy would fray Yeltsin's party even further.

Berezovsky did not believe there was any other choice. If he could make peace with Gusinsky, together they would control almost all of the television in the country, and most of the print media and journalists as well. Such a force launching continual, positive stories about Yeltsin while firing off negative innuendo about the Communists would have an enormous effect on popular perception. Further, if they could bring together the leading Oligarchs—the seven biggest, whom Berezovsky had already labeled in his head the Seven Bankers, though they had fingers in many, many industries—Berezovsky knew there would be enough money to run a truly Western-style campaign.

Chubais had already shown himself to be a strong leader in conversations at Davos, and the Oligarchs loved him for what he had done—creating a privatization system, shifting state businesses into the hands of the financiers. They would rally behind Chubais, and all that was needed was for Yeltsin to understand that this was the only way—the correct way—to win.

Berezovsky remained silent and seated, in that Alpine hideaway, feeling the warmth from the fire behind him, breathing that rarefied air. But his desperation began to shift into something else. Despite what George Soros might have thought, Berezovsky believed he could pull this off. He would save Russia, win an election—and, most important, safeguard his way of life.

CHAPTER TWELVE

June 19, 1996,

Logovaz Club

A SCANT FOUR MONTHS AFTER Davos, the world felt like it had shifted on its axis—again—and Berezovsky had never felt more alive, pinballing through the top floor of his club while campaign workers pirouetted around him at full speed, a veritable army of young men and women continuously shuttling between the Logovaz, Yeltsin's Presidential Club, and Chubais headquarters at the Kremlin.

The political race was going better than Berezovsky could have dreamed. And even better than that, he believed he was finally on the verge of achieving the goal he had set for himself after the assassination attempt back in 1994. The most profitable and important business, he had told anyone who would listen, was politics. Through politics, he was rising like a phoenix from the flames of that bombing. And he was doing it by creating a unique marriage of finance and politics.

Berezovsky grabbed a freshly printed campaign poster off a nearby velvet-lined counter, and held it aloft toward Badri Patarkatsishvili, his Georgian partner and best friend, sitting comfortably in a leather divan beneath one of the club's many large-screen televisions, smoking a cigar. Berezovsky poked at the picture on the front of the poster—an image of the Communist presidential candidate over a slogan that read, "This may be your last chance to buy food."

"Subtle," Badri laughed. Then he gestured toward the television set.

"Been switching back and forth between ORT and Gusinsky's NTV. From all the coverage, you'd think that Yeltsin was running against Stalin himself. By the next round of voting, people will be thinking about bread lines and gulags."

Berezovsky grinned. The turnaround in the popular opinion about the two candidates was already historic. Two days earlier, Yeltsin had registered almost thirty-four percent of the vote against less than thirty-three percent for the Communist candidate. The third-place candidate, General Lebed, had received less than fifteen percent—and had summarily resigned from the election, joining Yeltsin's campaign. His addition to their side was an incredible boost, as he was a well-respected military leader, with the sort of strength of character that appealed to the Russian nature.

It had taken a deal with the devil—or, more accurately, seven of them—but the "Davos Pact" that Berezovsky, through Chubais, had achieved, was functioning perfectly. Swallowing his own anger and animosity toward Gusinsky hadn't been easy; but there was no question that the banker and media magnate had been an enormous part of the equation. The journalists who worked for NTV were very well respected, and when they told the public that a return to communism would mean a return to the dark ages of Stalin and abject poverty, people listened.

Meanwhile, Berezovsky's gang of bankers had provided Chubais with an almost limitless war chest. The numbers were debatable, but

Berezovsky believed that together they had spent in the hundreds of millions on the campaign—more than any American president had ever spent to get elected. The voting was still close, and there would be a runoff, but Berezovsky now felt confident that Yeltsin would prevail. And when he did, Berezovsky knew, he and the other Oligarchs were going to benefit enormously. Between them, they already accounted for almost fifty percent of the nation's GDP. Seven men, with the wealth of half a country in their hands—and they were in the process of buying not just an election but a government.

Of course, such a statement would be a dangerous thing to say out loud. But Berezovsky had never been particularly good at limiting himself, controlling what he said. Already, his newest business colleague—Roman Abramovich, whom he now thought of as his protégé—was worried about being publicly associated with Berezovsky's political ambitions and machinations. Abramovich felt that the image of a man involved in the formation of Sibneft, essentially attempting to fix the election, could reflect badly on the company. To that end, they'd had a number of conversations about Berezovsky backing away from any public associations with the oil concern. Berezovsky had happily agreed; the truth was, he had no managerial interests, in fact he knew nothing about running an oil company and had no reason to be involved in any of its operations. His skill set had been in getting the thing off the ground, getting it privatized, and protecting its interests through what he was doing for Yeltsin. Account ledgers, business decisions, the corporate day-to-day—these held no interest for him.

As long as the money kept pouring in—as long as the deliveries of suitcases, carryalls, and envelopes full of American dollars kept arriving at the Logovaz Club to prop up ORT—and Berezovsky's increasingly lavish lifestyle—he was content. So far, Abramovich had made good on every request Berezovsky had made; a million here, five million there. Berezovsky wasn't certain how much the man had already sent him, but it had to be well over thirty million dollars. And there would be much, much more to come. Berezovsky didn't care what his official association with Sibneft might be—as long as the money kept flowing.

Abramovich was efficient and reliable. More than that, Berezovsky had grown to truly like the young man on a social level. They had vacationed together, dined together, celebrated each other's birthdays all over the world. The young man was ambitious, as Berezovsky had first perceived, but shy in public, choosing to eschew the limelight and keep himself out of the press at all costs. In fact, the public had begun to refer to him as the secret Oligarch—a man whose picture had never been taken, an invisible, rising star. Abramovich didn't care what the public thought; he simply wanted to grow his business, his empire.

In a few more days, Berezovsky was confident that the election would give Abramovich all the protection he needed to continue moving forward. Yeltsin was going to win, and the payoff for the men who supported him would be unprecedented.

Berezovsky was about to reach for another poster from his propaganda department to titillate Badri—when he was suddenly interrupted by a frantic commotion coming from the other end of the floor. He looked up in time to see his young, annoying assistant, Ivan, rushing toward him, holding a cordless phone. The bodyguards around Ivan looked terrified—obviously something important was happening. Berezovsky's first fear was that Yeltsin had suffered another heart attack; the old man had already endured four that Berezovsky knew of. Hell, it was hard enough battling Communists, but even Berezovsky was going to have difficulty coming up with a scheme to battle against the failure of Yeltsin's own heart. But as Ivan reached him and began to speak, Berezovsky realized the problem wasn't with Yeltsin's heart at all—but with his right hand.

"They've been arrested," Ivan sputtered, as he skidded to a stop in front of his boss. "Chubais's men, they were coming out of the White House with a cardboard box. The security agents are report-ing that the box had more than half a million dollars inside. Cash, no receipts, no papers."

"Security agents? Whose security agents?"

Ivan finally calmed down enough to clearly explain the situa-tion. It appeared that Korzhakov had made his move. His private security forces had arrested two of Chubais's campaign assistants, carrying a box of cash on their way out of the Russian White House.

A bold and terrifying move. Even, possibly, the precursor to a coup. Korzhakov had to know that Chubais wouldn't stand for his men being arrested, no matter what the charge. And to do such a thing in public, in the middle of the election?

"Arkady Yevstafyev and Sergei Lisovsky," Ivan continued. "They're being held at gunpoint right this minute. But they still seem to have their cell phones, and they've spoken to Chubais. General Lebed is already on his way to get them released."

Berezovsky shook his head. He looked at Badri, but his friend's face was unreadable behind his cigar. Korzhakov was obviously growing desperate. A month earlier, he'd been all talk, even though he had raised many hackles when he had made a statement implying that he thought the election would lead to a civil war—and that it should be canceled. Now it seemed as though he was attempting to start that civil war himself.

The charges themselves didn't matter. Hell, with the amount of money Berezovksy and the Oligarchs were pouring into the campaign, you could throw a rock at any man walking out of the White House and knock over a box filled with cash. Korzhakov was attempting to escalate the battle for Yeltsin's favor—and this time, Berezovsky believed, the man had gone too far.

Berezovsky grabbed the phone from Ivan's hand. It was time to circle the wagons. He intended to call everyone he could; Chubais, he was informed, was already on his way over. They would gather at the Logovaz and wait out the night; it was as safe a place as they could find. But Berezovsky knew that in this moment, the most important member of their group wouldn't be an Oligarch or a campaign manager.

Money and ideology were powerful cards—but a president's daughter trumped everything.

The minute Berezovsky heard Tatiana's voice on the other end of the line, he knew that one way or another, the Korzhakov situation would soon be resolved.

◆　◆　◆

By 3:30 in the morning, the air in the club still rang with the voices of some of the most powerful and wealthy men in Russia—but the edge of fear that had gripped Berezovsky earlier had begun to recede. Tatiana had already visited and left. Badri was still sitting beneath the television, watching the screen even more intently. General Lebed, on Chubais's behalf, had made a number of appearances over the airwaves already—speaking directly to the cameras: "It appears that somebody is trying to disrupt the elections. Any attempt at mutiny will be put down mercilessly."

Intense words. Berezovsky's cheeks had heated up as he had watched the general speak, and he had been able to see from Badri's expression that the situation was reaching an end.

Berezovsky had only heard one side of the phone calls between Tatiana and her father, but he was certain that, as of tomorrow morning, Korzhakov would be finished. More than that, he believed that Yeltsin was going to fire three of his previously most powerful confidants: Korzhakov, with whom he had shared vodka, climbed onto tanks, and run a country; Mikhail Barsukov, current head of the FSB, who had presumably allowed these arrests to happen and was a big supporter of Korzhakov's; and Oleg Soskovets, the deputy prime minister, a former Red Director from the steel industry, as right-wing as they came.

It would be enormously painful for the president, but it would send a clear pro-democracy message. Yeltsin wasn't going to take the election by force; he was going to take it by vote. The loss of Korzhakov would hurt Yeltsin deeply, but it might very well ensure his victory.

With Korzhakov gone, Berezovsky and his Oligarchs would find themselves in an even stronger position. Berezovksy's role in the Family would become more integral, and he would be closer to Yeltsin than ever. He might even be involved in the search for someone to fill the vacuum at the head of the FSB. Yeltsin would be looking for someone exceedingly loyal, a true yes-man, a cog who knew when to turn, when to stay still.

But that was something for tomorrow, and the days after that. For the moment, Berezovsky could clear his mind of such things, and allow himself to relax. Badri lit another cigar.

The Georgian was right.

It was time to celebrate.

PART TWO

Two bears can't live in one cave.

—OLD RUSSIAN PROVERB

CHAPTER THIRTEEN

December 1997,

FSB Headquarters, Lubyanka Square

IN RETROSPECT, ALEXANDER LITVINENKO realized, he should have known that something out of the ordinary was about to happen the minute he entered the stark, cement-walled office on the third floor of the mammoth building. Nine fifteen a.m., and the briefing was already in full swing. Three other agents were gathered in the room, two of them seated on institutional-style metal folding chairs, a third leaning against the far wall next to a heavy wooden bookshelf, overflowing with legal texts, police procedure manuals, and unmarked suspect files. At the front of the room, seated at the heavy wooden desk by the only window, in unusually good humor—his departmental superior. The man was laughing heartily, at the tail end of a joke that Litvinenko had no intention of asking him to repeat.

After the fact, Litvinenko might have guessed that his normally finely tuned awareness of the world around him had been dulled by a surprisingly long period of normality—if such a word could ever have been appropriate in the life of a secret service agent. Yet, in the eighteen months since the election that had secured his patron Berezovsky's position for the foreseeable future, Litvinenko's world had slid into a pleasant rhythm; days spent working for the FSB on numerous investigations involving the gangsters who continued to battle it out on the streets of Moscow, and early evenings often spent meeting with Berezovsky at the Logovaz Club to discuss matters that made Litvinenko feel he was a part of an elite world of wealth and power.

Certainly, Berezovsky's stock was riding high. Berezovsky had been appointed the deputy secretary of national security, perhaps as a reward for the election that he had massaged toward victory, and he had suddenly found himself involved in the conflict between the Russian Federation and the Republic of Chechnya, which was almost universally opposed by the Russian public. But that conflict seemed to be heading toward some sort of resolution.

Of course, Litvinenko knew better than anyone that Berezovsky was his own best propagandist. The stories he told in their evening sessions grew more extravagant the more the vodka flowed—or the more ears were turned in the Oligarch's direction. These stories ranged from the merely humorous to the fabulously extreme—from tales of Berezovsky single-handedly saving Yeltsin, democracy, and capitalism, to stories about his rapidly growing portfolio of businesses—Sibneft, ORT, and now Aeroflot, the national airline—to narratives that seemed so insane it was impossible to know if they could be true—such as the story of Berezovsky rescuing, again single-handedly, a group of hostages held by Chechen rebels by showing up in person on his private jet, and trading the poor civilians' safety for a hundred-thousand-dollar Patek Philippe watch.

It was certain that Berezovsky did have relations with the Chechens; but Litvinenko suspected that most of the conversations with the terrorists had involved Badri, the Georgian, who had the proper "demeanor" for dealing with the type of men who wore Kalashnikov rifles to business meetings. Whatever the case, Berezovsky was riding high—and that meant Litvinenko was also living well. Berezovsky had never been richer; his wealth had been estimated to be close to three billion dollars, though nobody knew for certain. Directly after the elections, Abramovich's oil company had sprung up in value by, some said, more than a factor of twenty. Berezovsky, in turn, was receiving payments on an almost weekly basis. It seemed that all he needed to do was pick up the phone and dial, and a suitcase would arrive filled with US dollars. For his part, Litvinenko understood that sort of business relationship; after all, Berezovsky could pick up the phone and dial him, too, and Litvinenko would hurry straight to his office—his FSB badge in one hand, his automatic in the other.

But ever since Vlad Listyev's murder, so long ago, Litvinenko hadn't needed to draw his weapon even once at Berezovsky's behest. Now that Korzhakov was gone and Tatiana Yeltsin seemed squarely in Berezovsky's camp, Berezovsky himself had the most powerful krysha of all. In fact, he had solidified his position with the Family even further by hiring Yeltsin's son-in-law to run Aeroflot. Litvinenko had begun to believe that the only thing bigger than Boris Berezovsky's delusions of grandeur was Boris Berezovsky's actual life.

Litvinenko's life might not have been quite as grand—but it was certainly happy. He and his ballroom dancer were well provided for, and he saw most of what he did for the FSB in basically noble terms. The world around them was still gripped by chaos, but he was essentially a beat cop, and his job was to try to clean up as much of the mess as he could.

Sometimes, of course, that meant the application of violent methods; Litvinenko had recently been promoted into a group of officers tasked with dealing with organized crime in a particularly intense way, which meant that, whenever he read about a graphic and spectacular murder that had taken place in the streets of Moscow—a bomb going off in a café or a businessman found hanging from a bridge without his hands and feet—Litvinenko and his colleagues might need to "get a little rough" in the quest to solve the crime. But he still believed that, each night, he came home with clean hands.

As he slid into the third-floor office, and took the one empty chair, just a few feet from the edge of his superior's vast desk—he suddenly wondered if that was about to change.

When his superior stopped laughing, he seemed to focus directly on Litvinenko. The man was still smiling, but his words had lost any tinge of humor.

"So your friend has been coming up in conversation."

The other agents shifted uncomfortably in their chairs. The lead officer continued—but didn't get to a name until a few sentences into his monologue.

"I'm right, aren't I? Boris Berezovsky is your friend, correct?"

Litvinenko did not meet the man's eyes, instead glancing toward the nearest cement wall. He felt an inadvertent shiver, looking at the smooth, hard material. He knew well the history of this building. The precisely rectangular, many-storied, fortified structure rose up above the northeastern corner of Lubyanka Square like some sort of unholy behemoth—and for most Russians, the sight of even the building's shadow sent daggers up the spine. In Stalin's era, this was an address you didn't want to hear mention of, let alone approach. The first floor contained one of the most feared prisons in Russia, Lubyanka, where many of the nation's worst enemies and most famous revolutionaries had been held, tortured, and sometimes killed. Hundreds, if not thousands, of Stalin's nemeses had ended up there—just two floors below where Litvinenko was now sitting. There was an old joke that he had often heard—that this had once been the tallest building in Russia, because you could see Siberia from its basement.

Litvinenko had no doubt that these walls could tell stories that would terrify even the most hardened FSB agent. But his superior, at the moment, was still all smiles—even as he spoke words, as Litvinenko would later remember them, that sent the young agent into a sudden and severe state of shock.

"Boris Berezovsky, you know, the Jew." And then the man stood and placed his hands flat against his desk. "You should kill him."

Litvinenko looked at his colleagues in their metal chairs, but they would not meet his eyes. He was certain they had all heard it—but the words seemed so strange, impossible, said so conversationally, as if they were just another normal bit of dialogue. But in his mind, there could be no doubt of their meaning: Litvinenko was being given an order. It was not the first order he had been given by this man that he had seen as wrong. He had been asked to take part in rough interrogations, in a handful of beatings, that sort of thing—but this was insane and extreme.

"Mr. Berezovsky is my associate," he began trying to put into words some sort of response that would get him out of the situation, "I've known him for some time—"

"Yes," the man interrupted. "He is your friend, your employer. And he is causing problems for many people, and has been a problem for this country for a long time, and he should be dealt with."

Litvinenko knew that Berezovsky had made many enemies over the past few years, both in business and in politics. But this conversation, these orders—as Litvinenko saw them—why were they coming now? And why to him? The FSB deny that any conversation of this kind took place.

He had never thought of his superior as an overly complicated thinker. Perhaps he had chosen to involve Litvinenko because he thought the young agent's association with the Oligarch would make the job easy. And since Litvinenko was considered a loyal FSB agent, his superior probably did not think he would choose a businessman, with no FSB ties, over an order. But such a murder? An assassination like this—it was exactly the sort of thing he was supposed to be fighting against. He did not consider himself some sort of hero, but he drew lines, he had always drawn lines. And Berezovsky was his friend, his patron, his supporter. His krysha.

Litvinenko sat in silence, trying to figure out what he should say. He could tell the other agents were struggling not to watch him, but they were waiting to hear how he would respond. He thought again about that prison on the first floor of the building—and the days of the past when men who said the wrong thing to a superior might very well have ended up standing in front of cement walls just like those that surrounded him.

For the moment, he decided to say nothing, to give no response at all. But inside, he was already coming to a conclusion. A rift was opening, a chasm so deep he couldn't see the bottom, and he felt like he was in danger of falling right in. He knew, once again, he needed to make a decision that would affect the rest of his life.

A decision that might very well land him at the bottom of that chasm, for good.

CHAPTER FOURTEEN

March 1998,

Alexandrovka Dacha, Podolsk District

FOR A BRIEF MOMENT, Litvinenko felt himself shrink against the cream-colored couch, vanishing into the cushions as he stared at the dead, glossy, pitch-black eye of the video camera, because in his mind, he wasn't looking into the lens of a video recording device, which was standing on a metallic tripod in a corner of the living room of Boris Berezovsky's state-financed country estate outside Moscow—instead he was looking right into the barrel of a gun, pointed directly between his eyes.

Marina was just a few feet away, nervously watching him, waiting for him to speak; he knew she supported what he was doing, even though it terrified her. She supported him because she believed in him, and the way he thought, and the decisions he had made. And next to her, Berezovsky himself, moving back and forth on the balls of his feet, real anger in his face. Berezovsky supported Litvinenko, as well, but for many different reasons. Fury, revenge, strategy— these were the things that moved behind the businessman's pinpoint eyes. Litvinenko cared little for any of these emotions; this was not a strategy any more than suicide might be—and yet he felt it was the only thing he could do, the only choice he had.

On the couch next to him were two other FSB agents, colleagues with just as much to lose, taking the same chances as Litvinenko—but speaking because they also felt they had no other choice. The videotaping session was being done in secret—something Berezovsky called an insurance policy. The plan was not yet to go public with the accusations about the assassination orders: this tape itself would be a weapon with which they could threaten the powers above Litvinenko at the FSB to make changes, and back off from such behavior. Litvinenko had convinced himself that what he was doing wasn't a betrayal, but rather, an attempt to change the organization for the better.

Finally, staring into that lens, Litvinenko found his voice. He began to tell the story of how he had been ordered to kill his patron. The other agents chimed in as well, adding their own voices when necessary. Across from them sat one of ORT's best-known journalists, host of a popular show, who acted as interviewer.

The order to assassinate Berezovsky was not the only topic covered. Among the agents, they had witnessed other actions they considered overreaching. One of the agents spoke about a kidnapping plot involving a political agitator. Another spoke of a setup involving a different FSB agent. The words one of the men used—"The reasons we have gotten you out of bed are that these actions are against the law, against the criminal code, and are not moral"—seemed to sum up Litvinenko's own thoughts, and the impetus for the dangerous decision he had made.

He could feel Marina watching him, nodding slowly as he spoke. *I do understand,* he said, *that an officer is not supposed to give interviews on television—but I realize the time has come. I wouldn't do what I do now . . . but I fear for the life of my child and my wife.*

The camera continued to roll. Litvinenko was melded into the couch, but he could see that Berezovsky was leaning forward, almost on his toes.

If nothing is done, if this lawlessness were to continue, it would ruin the country.

Litvinenko knew that now he had gone past the point of no return.

He had saved Berezovsky's life, but perhaps at enormous cost. Berezovsky's plan was dangerous: Berezovsky intended to go to the FSB, lodge a formal complaint, and use his power with Yeltsin to make the FSB listen to what he had to say. He had promised to protect Litvinenko, but Litvinenko was not naïve enough to think that Berezovsky would risk his own safety or position for a young agent. Which meant that things could easily spiral out of control.

Berezovsky would know the right people to talk to, and with this tape as his weapon, heads would certainly roll, maybe at even the highest levels of the FSB. But a new man would be brought in to find replacements for them. Whoever took control would have Litvinenko's fate in his hands. Litvinenko could only hope that such a man would understand.

CHAPTER FIFTEEN

November 11, 1998,

FSB Headquarters, Lubyanka Square

MOVING THROUGH THE CORRIDORS of the third floor of that damned ominous building, Berezovsky felt a bit of annoyance as he listened to the heavy breathing of the young agent who was chugging along next to him, nervously clutching a binder of evidence under his arm. Litvinenko was acting as if he were on his way to the gallows, when in fact he was really on his way into history. He'd blown the loudest whistle in agency history, and Berezovsky was proud of his employee and friend. Now Litvinenko just needed to keep his head up and trust Berezovsky. After all, Berezovsky was at the height of his powers.

Winning the election for Yeltsin had been a monumental feat; this next task was simply fixing a flaw that ran like a structural crack down the center of the largest security agency in the world. And he had already accomplished much. Since secretly videotaping Litvinenko and the other agents, he had worked through his contacts to get rid of many of the most corrupt elements in the FSB. That had included replacing the head of the agency with a man he believed would be more acquiescent to the realities of the new regime. And now he was bringing Litvinenko to meet face-to-face with this new director, to put this issue to rest.

Personally, he wasn't sure that presenting the man with a binder of evidence was the best strategy. Starting off a meeting by handing the new head man a stack of notations about the flaws of the previous leadership wouldn't be particularly productive. The new head would have his own way of doing things; the only important thing was that he like you.

To that end, Berezovsky believed he was already ahead of the game. He had been instrumental in putting the man in that third-floor, corner office.

"Sasha," he said to Litvinenko, using his nickname, as they were now close friends. "You need to do something about your face. You don't look like you're meeting your new boss. You look like you're heading to a funeral."

Litvinenko tried to smile, but he was obviously nervous. When they reached the office, Berezovsky didn't wait for Litvinenko to knock—he simply reached for the knob.

The young man on the other side of the sparsely decorated office hopped up out of his chair with the grace of a natural athlete, ushering the two of them inside with a friendly but spare wave of his hand. He wasn't exactly smiling, but his narrow face was amiable, his intelligent eyes taking them both in with rapid flicks, top to bottom. He wasn't tall, but he was obviously very fit, dressed immaculately, and he seemed to have taken to his new role with a confidence that impressed Berezovsky. This wasn't at all the minor functionary Berezovsky remembered. When Berezovsky had met this man years earlier, he was little more than an assistant.

At the time, Berezovsky had needed aid in setting up a car dealership in St. Petersburg, and the mayor of the city had handed him off to his deputy—a former long-term KGB officer by the name of Vladimir Putin. Berezovsky had been impressed immediately by the young man's efficiency, and at a dinner party, he had learned a bit more about the man's background. A child of poverty, like so many in Russia, Putin had grown up for a time in a communal apartment. He hadn't been a wonderful student, but he was an impressive athlete who had gone on to become a judo champion. After stints studying law and language, he had matriculated right into the KGB, and had then put in more than sixteen years as a dutiful agent. His main job had apparently been analyzing foreign agents and trying to turn them. He had been stationed in Germany, where he'd married, had a couple of daughters, and then come back home to work at the University of St. Petersburg for a former teacher—who, in turn, was elected mayor of the city. And even though Putin had spent so much time in the security agency, he had democratic leanings; in 1991, when Yeltsin took power and communism fell, he left the KGB.

His ascension to the head of the FSB had come on the heels of being brought to Moscow by Yeltsin and the Family. Berezovsky had been privy to that decision; the most important characteristics Yeltsin had been looking for in appointments had been loyalty, efficiency, and strength—and these were things that defined the former KGB man. When Putin's boss, the mayor, had lost his own election in 1996, Putin had the opportunity to work for the winning party. Instead, he resigned, remaining loyal to his mentor. That meant more to Berezovsky than all the efficiency in the world. When you were placing a man in a position of power, you wanted someone who was loyal in the best meaning of the word—you wanted a perfect cog. Berezovsky firmly believed Putin to be that perfect cog; a strongman who could be controlled, who could see the importance of not making waves.

Which was exactly why Berezovsky had brought Litvinenko to meet with Putin, now that he was the new head of the FSB. First, Berezovsky had written a letter, demanding that the FSB address the assassination order—but he had felt the extra step of bringing his whistle-blower to meet with the new head of the agency would be icing on the cake. He felt sure Putin would show them the respect they deserved.

After the brief introductions were over, Putin ushered them to their seats in front of his desk. As Berezovsky had remembered from the brief encounter in St. Petersburg, Putin was not a man for idle chitchat. He quickly steered the conversation to Litvinenko's claims and the stack of evidence the young agent had brought with them. Putin then immediately assured Berezovsky that he was taking the charges very seriously, not simply because his predecessor had lost his job, but because he was a man who believed in law and order. But Berezovsky could also see, in the way Putin avoided looking at the young agent, from the way he skimmed through the evidence without any sense of shock or disgust about what he was seeing, that his years with the KGB had made him inherently suspicious of a man who had turned on the security agency.

Putin finished the meeting on a high note, telling them both he would look into these things, and if he found any more issues that needed to be dealt with, he would make sure the right things were done.

Even so, it wasn't until Berezovsky and Litvinenko were out in the hallway, Putin's door shut behind them, that the young agent seemed to relax, if only a fraction, loosening his shoulders beneath his jeans jacket. Berezovsky could tell that Litvinenko was waging an inner battle with himself, wondering if he had done the right thing, wondering if this new FSB director was really going to make an effort to root out the bad elements in his agency—or instead root out the agent who had blown the whistle in the first place.

Berezovsky, for his part, was waging no inner war. The Oligarch wasn't going to leave these things to chance or fate or faith, or even to the efficient, loyal cog who Yeltsin and the Family had pulled from the wilds of St. Petersburg. Berezovsky had a plan. If the FSB did not act immediately to finish cleaning up its own mess, Berezovsky intended to force its hand.

November 17, 1998,
Interfax Press Center, Tverskaya Street, Moscow

Berezovsky watched with a choreographer's pride, as a palpable hush swept through the crowded conference room; the five men on the dais moved in a single file, choosing their seats behind a frenzied bloom of microphones from a dozen different news organizations—many of them owned by Berezovsky himself—and beneath the watchful eye of a pair of oversize television cameras. Flashbulbs went off like fireworks, and then the hush was replaced by an awed rumble, the gathered journalists jockeying with each other for a better view of the bizarre spectacle.

Four of the men on the dais were wearing black balaclavas, and two more had donned large, dark sunglasses. Only Litvinenko himself was unadorned, dressed in a jacket with a poorly matching tie.

He was without a mask or sunglasses not because of any sense of newfound fearlessness. He was out there, for the world to see, because the media had already identified him as the lead whistleblower, shortly after Berezovsky had published his own open letter to Vladimir Putin in the *Kommersant*, Berezovsky's newspaper—demanding that the FSB restore order and law to the security agency.

That letter had been published six days ago—but Berezovsky had come to the conclusion that the dramatic changes he was asking for demanded an even more dramatic presentation.

It hadn't been easy to convince Litvinenko and the other agents he had gathered to go public like this; but in the end, they had realized that the cameras and journalists provided much more security than a false anonymity. Did these men really think that those black masks would keep a determined FSB from exacting vengeance, if that was the route the agency intended to take? The men's only real option, in Berezovsky's opinion, was to go big and go public—an approach directly in Berezovsky's wheelhouse.

Concealing himself in a corner of the Interfax conference room, obscured by the shadows cast by the drawn shades of the long hall filled with row after row of journalists, Berezovsky listened as Litvinenko kicked off the conference—speaking carefully into the microphones, telling much the same story he had told in the private videotaping session, for the secret tape that Berezovsky still had in his possession. Detailing the orders to assassinate Berezovsky and a number of other wealthy businessmen, detailing kidnapping plots and any number of corrupt decrees from their superiors at the FSB. In the end, asking, begging Mr. Putin to clean up the agency.

In the circus-like atmosphere that Berezovsky had orchestrated, it was once again hard for the Oligarch not to marvel at the incredible changes in his fortune. Not four years earlier, when someone had attempted to take his life, he had been forced to slink off to Switzerland, wrapped up in bandages, a joke people pointed and laughed at, a man they called Smoky behind his back. Now here he was, a president in his pocket, waving a finger at the most-feared security agency in perhaps the world. How the FSB would eventually respond to Litvinenko's whistle-blowing was an unknown—many would certainly see such a public press conference as an embarrassment.

Whatever the fallout for the agents, Berezovsky was certain of one thing. The world would hear what Litvinenko had to say—and that meant that Berezovsky, himself, would be untouchable.

CHAPTER SIXTEEN

January 1999,

Krasnoyarsk, Siberia

THE MI-8 HELICOPTER BANKED low over the frozen landscape, tilting hard to the left as it narrowly avoided a sudden bristle of Siberian fir trees, rising up from the foot of a nearby cliff face. In the heated interior of the copter's leather-paneled cabin, Roman Abramovich tested his harness once again, while avoiding, as best he could, leaning with too much of his weight against the cold glass window to his side. Across the cabin, seated facing him, Badri Patarkatsishvili grinned from behind his thick, white mustache. If he thought for a moment that Abramovich was scared of either heights or unchecked velocity, he was mistaken; but being in a fifteen-year-old helicopter that hadn't seen zero degrees in months and was now flying through icy Arctic air was another story altogether.

Of course, Abramovich was no stranger to this frozen corner of Russia. He had grown up a long stone's throw from this section of Siberia, and he had built his trading business in the oil fields and refineries just a few stops down along the trans-Siberian railroad. The snowy, ice-covered mountains he could see on the horizon to his left, the thick, lush forests that seemed to rise up out of the ground like verdant brushstrokes across the permanently frozen tundra—these were as familiar to him as the heavy scent of burned oil coming from the helicopter's overtaxed, twin turbines.

"Over there," shouted Eugene, seated to Abramovich's right, hoping to be heard over the immense racket of the helicopter's rotors. "Another few hundred yards, past those trees."

The third man who had joined them on the short chopper ride from the center of the city of Krasnoyarsk, Eugene was Abramovich's most trusted employee, his business partner and right-hand man. He was the only man Abramovich would have dragged so far—the long trek from Moscow had taken them most of a day, and had involved a car, a private jet, and a train, not to mention this chopper—to contemplate something as crazy as the proposition that Badri, assuredly in partnership with Berezovsky, had proposed.

To be fair, Krasnoyarsk itself was a unique and beautiful place; a sort of jewel tucked away in the Siberian tundra, a glistening, rapidly modernizing city situated right on the twisting banks of the Yenisei River. Once upon a time, this area had held Stalin's gulags—prison camps out of every Russian's nightmares, grim places in the middle of a wilderness of icy mountains and wolf-ridden woods. But in modern times, Krasnoyarsk had transformed into a place of factories, mining corporations, oil concerns, and much more; one of the three largest metropolises in the entire region, after Novosibirsk and Omsk, the cities out of which Abramovich had built Sibneft.

"Now, that is something," Badri responded, jabbing a thick finger at the window, inches from Eugene's face. "Isn't it just as beautiful as I described?"

The Georgian wasn't talking about Krasnoyarsk, the trees, the cliffs, or the mountains. Abramovich glanced past his business associate Eugene at the low, barracks-like buildings that spread out in front of the helicopter for what appeared to be at least a quarter mile. There were low, windowless cubes and rectangles that could only be factories. Interspersed between them, smelting plants with smokestacks rising high enough to give the helicopter pilot something to test his skills against. High barbed wire topped chain-link fences around circular storage facilities and many parking lots full of flatbed trucks. Even train cars, lined up in sleek black rows, next to a very large open loading dock filled with gargantuan machinery.

But the most notable aspect of the view below was not the enormity of the factories, the smelting plants, the storage and loading facilities—it was the fact that those smokestacks were obviously dormant; no exhaust at all came from the giant plant. Abramovich guessed that the air outside the chopper was as crisp and clean as he remembered from his childhood, a wind gusting out of the Arctic Circle, cleansed by the river and the trees.

"I'm not sure I see anything beautiful about a dead factory," Abramovich responded, but his words just made Badri laugh even louder.

Abramovich had grown fond of the Georgian strongman. He was amiable and direct—and in many ways the most straightforward man Abramovich had ever met. He had a keen sense of humor, an ability to put people completely and immediately at ease; at the same time, something about him always meant business, and one look from him could send shards of terror down even a born mobster's spine. Even so, with Badri—unlike Berezovsky, who was impulsive, emotional, perhaps even bipolar—you always knew where you stood.

Over the past year and a half since the Sibneft "loans for shares" deal had been finalized, Abramovich and his right-hand man,

Eugene, had gotten to know the Georgian quite well—mainly because Berezovsky, their patron, had proven to possess an appetite for excess that even Abramovich had underestimated, the sort of ravenous hunger that made him think of a mythical beast from some Siberian fairy tale. Not a week had gone without a phone call requesting money for some escapade or another—sometimes involving ORT, but just as often involving some personal purchase that Berezovsky simply couldn't do without. Sometimes the call would come from Berezovsky himself, but more often, as the months progressed and the Oligarch became more and more caught up in his political machinations, the requests came through Badri; the Georgian would show up at the Sibneft offices, grinning widely behind his mustache. The demands for money ran from the banal—fifteen thousand dollars here, eighteen thousand dollars there—to the practically insane. Millions—one, two, ten—and usually it had to be right away, cash if possible. Often, the requests came without any description of what the money was going to be used for, but sometimes Badri would explain what it was that Berezovsky so desperately needed.

In the beginning, it was payments to keep ORT afloat; but since the election in 1996, the focus seemed to shift to keeping Berezovsky's lifestyle intact. The money had gone to purchase rare works of art for the Oligarch's homes and offices; to settle girlfriends' credit card bills; to help pay for at least one yacht, a private airplane, and even three French châteaus in the Antibes. All of it under the table, without any papers being filled out or contracts being signed. Just a phone call or a visit from Badri, followed by a suitcase full of money. There was no real paper trail, but if Abramovich had to calculate it, he believed that, in 1996 alone, he had paid at least thirty million to his krysha. In 1997, it had to be closer to fifty million. In 1998, maybe seventy or eighty million more. So much money, in such a crazy fashion: at Sibneft, they had simply begun to refer to the payments as Project Boris, which everyone accepted, if reluctantly, as the price of doing business.

It was a frustrating arrangement. At times, Abramovich had considered attempting to slow or stop the flow of cash—but the realities of the market and the business environment made any attempt to cut off ties with Berezovsky risky, if not outright suicidal. Without the Oligarch's continued connections to the Kremlin and to the Family, Sibneft would not have existed—and there was always the chance that, without Berezovsky, the company would suddenly find itself out of the good graces of the Yeltsin government. The higher Berezovsky rose, the greater his political status and, the thinking went, the better it was for Sibneft.

Abramovich simply had to accept that, often, he was writing checks that had more to do with inflating the entity known as Boris Berezovsky more than any particular business concern. One of the oddest expenditures in the past few months, and one that still irked him, had to do with Berezovsky's role in the Chechen conflict. As the story went, after Chechen terrorists had kidnapped a pair of Brits from the capital city of Grozny in July of the year before, the Russian government had spent months trying to negotiate their release. Nothing was working, until the white knight Boris Berezovsky stepped in, like a superhero out of a Hollywood movie, making some sort of deal with the terrorists—then flying the hostages out to freedom on his own private jet.

In reality, most of the negotiations with the Chechens had most likely involved Badri more than Berezovsky. And for certain, the private jet had been paid for by Sibneft—and Roman Abramovich. The ransom that had freed the aid workers had also been paid by Sibneft—and Roman Abramovich.

But Abramovich had never wanted any press or even acknowledgment for his involvement; he had always been happy to stay out of the limelight that Berezovsky craved.

Over the past few years, the two men had developed an intricate relationship—built around payments—but also one that mimicked an actual friendship. They celebrated holidays together, spending New Year's in the Caribbean, birthdays at the Logovaz Club and in the châteaus in France and in chalets in Switzerland; they had spent time on various yachts, on beaches on Mallorca and the Riviera. But Abramovich had also spent countless hours waiting in the anteroom outside Berezovsky's office, like some sort of assistant, at the older man's beck and call. Berezovsky certainly did not consider him an equal—and what sort of real friendship could be built on an unequal footing?

Nor was he exactly a business partner; Berezovsky had nothing to do with the day-to-day business of the oil company, and Abramovich doubted the man could read a balance sheet if his life depended on it. Berezovsky knew how to work the Kremlin, knew how to leverage friendships and political power to make things happen—and he knew how to use a telephone to ask for money. His only other truly impressive skill was that he knew, better than most, how to spot and take advantage of opportunities.

"You see a dead factory," Badri responded, his deep voice like a sonic boom. "I see an invaluable asset, that is getting cheaper by the day."

Even though it was Badri who had accompanied them on this Siberian excursion, Abramovich had no doubt that it was Berezovsky who had come up with the idea, having spotted yet another opportunity.

From what Abramovich understood, the situation had come about due to Berezovsky's on-again, off-again relationship with General Lebed—the military man who had been the third-place finisher in the 1996 election before going over to Yeltsin's team. Lebed, as a reward for his support of Yeltsin, had been made governor of this entire Siberian province, a resource-rich but far-flung section of the country that seemed always to be engulfed in some sort of labor or economic turmoil. Case in point—the dead factory below had only days ago been one of the largest production facilities of aluminum in the world—now frozen in place because of a labor dispute that had erupted in one of the biggest strikes in recent history.

Abramovich could still picture the crowds of angry, striking workers, the largest of which they had flown directly over during the short chopper ride to the factory. The laborers had effectively shut down a large swath of Krasnoyarsk; their demands were confusing, but had to do with better pay, safer conditions, fairer hours. Every minute they were on the streets, the aluminum industry took a major hit—but, to be sure, strikes were only one facet of the ugliness that revolved around the multibillion-dollar business of one of the most utilized and useful metals in the modern world. Abramovich was well aware—aluminum was a dirty business. The press in Moscow even had a name for the chaos that had been tearing through the industry over the past twelve months: the Aluminum Wars. A staggering number of murders had been committed in a short period of time, as different businessmen jockeyed for control, amid the labor issues, privatization attempts, and general pricing confusion. Abramovich had even read that there was a murder every three days that had to do with aluminum—from shootings in restaurants and bars to full-out gun battles at smelting plants.

In fact, the giant, dormant factory they were now flying over was run by a man who was notorious for terrifying his competitors. Between the manager's arrest and the strikes, the company was now in complete disarray.

Chaos, murder, mayhem—and obviously, in Berezovsky and Badri's opinion, opportunity.

When the Georgian had first approached Abramovich with the idea of throwing their hat into the aluminum industry's ring, Abramovich had turned him down flat. He told Badri that it was madness, that they didn't need this sort of trouble. But Badri had persisted, saying how much money could be made if someone were to succeed in unifying the industry under one company—much as Abramovich had done with Sibneft.

Eventually, Abramovich had looked again at the situation, and then had shown the numbers to Eugene, one of the most brilliant business minds around. Together, they agreed that Badri was right, in a fashion. If they could figure out a way to navigate the dangerous waters of the metal's production, consolidate the foundries, take care of the strikes—there would be an enormous amount of profit to be made. The key would be to convince the rival groups that it would be much more profitable and productive to make deals with each other—rather than try to kill each other. Two particularly vicious groups had to be dealt with, but Badri believed he could talk to them in terms they would understand. If they needed to lock the competing gangs in a room overnight, demand that they make a deal and come out millionaires or murder each other there on the spot—well, that's what they would do. In the end, Badri believed, everyone's goal was the same—to make as much money as possible.

As for the strikes, the labor situation, the politics—no doubt General Lebed would be pleased if someone could move in and get the strikers off his streets. His relationship with Berezovsky was like the wind—you never knew which way it was going to blow. But he would be helpful, if he believed they could actually achieve some sort of unification that would stop the murders and clean up his region.

In terms of consolidating the industry, Abramovich had an ace up his sleeve: a young man named Oleg Deripaska, who had grown up in similar circumstances as Abramovich—a kid from a poor region surrounding the Black Sea. Deripaska had worked his way from the factory floor in the metal business, and had built himself into a major player in the industry. Along the way, he had survived numerous assassination attempts and violent threats—at one point, a threat to him personally had been followed by one of his managers being shot twice. Even so, he had maintained his position at the top of the business, paying off huge krysha bills to various local figures to keep his factories running smoothly, although Deripaska denies any impropriety or association with anything illicit or illegal.

Abramovich had gotten to know Deripaska well, and most of his knowledge of the aluminum industry came through hearing the stories Deripaska told. Abramovich had begun to believe that, with Deripaska's involvement, a consolidation might be possible.

"Five hundred and fifty million," Badri continued, still looking out the helicopter window. "You could free a lot of British aide workers for that sort of money, but I think the return on investment is much higher here."

The number was approximately what Eugene, Abramovich, and Deripaska had come up with—the amount it would take to buy their way into aluminum with enough of a bankroll to make all the elements happy enough to join together and stop killing each other. The arrangement had been made during a twelve-hour, all-night marathon session. Abramovich and Eugene had brought all the elements together in a room, and had essentially locked the doors until 6:00 a.m. the next morning. Deripaska and the other aluminum magnates essentially had to make a choice—continue killing each other over the metal industry, or settle down, stop the fighting, and make a ton of money together. In the end, the weight—both financial and political—that Abramovich and his connections brought to the table pushed everyone to make the deal—and put an end to the Aluminum Wars. Furthermore, Eugene had come up with a sophisticated, genius scheme to allow them to conjure up the more than half a billion dollars necessary without actually laying down the cash themselves: they would merge the different aluminum elements, and then use the new company's assets to cover the payment.

All of it worked out without anyone firing a shot: end the wars, solve the strikes, and put another billion-dollar asset under their umbrella.

Whatever Abramovich truly thought of Boris Berezovsky, he had an eye for opportunities—even if other people had to figure out how to mine them for their value. And as long as the Oligarch stayed important and close to the people in charge of the government—as long as he was entrenched with the Family—he had the connections necessary to let people like Abramovich do what they did best in a safe, productive environment.

The question was, how long could Berezovsky remain such an important player—extending himself further and further, embroiling himself in drama after drama, controversy after controversy? Business in Russia was cutthroat—the Aluminum Wars were a prime example—but the political world could be equally, if not more, dangerous. Yeltsin, for all that he had done, was a sick, aging man—he wasn't going to last forever.

Abramovich could only hope that whoever eventually took the president's place could tolerate a man like Boris Berezovsky as Yeltsin obviously had. It took a special sort of demeanor to accept such a dramatic presence, hovering like a sputtering, loud, old helicopter around his head.

CHAPTER SEVENTEEN

November 27, 1999,

Moscow

A FEW MINUTES PAST NOON on a crisp November afternoon, one year and ten days from the bizarre and ill-fated whistle-blowing press conference—which the media and the public had written off as a dramatic farce orchestrated by Berezovsky for his own personal enlargement—Alexander Litvinenko was receiving a hard lesson in the relativity of time.

The cracked skin of his wrists rubbed raw against the cold metal of handcuffs, his body thin and pale beneath a stiff prison uniform, his shoulders hunched forward as he folded his lanky body into the narrow defendant's docket of a crowded courtroom, he was wading through what felt like forever—the longest four hours imaginable, as the judge, still in his chambers somewhere on the other side of the courtroom walls, deliberated his fate. Although Litvinenko remained facing forward, he knew that behind him, in row after row of seats in the tightly controlled courtroom, were journalists, cameramen, television reporters. They had come for another spectacle, this time arranged by the state instead of an Oligarch.

Litvinenko had been fired from his job with the FSB back in January. His dismissal had merited only a sentence or two in the local newspapers. But when he had been unceremoniously arrested on an uncharacteristically cold, snowy day in March, dragged away from his home to Lefortovo Prison—famous for formerly having been the KGB's jail—he had ended up in a paragraph on the front page, with supporting photos. The charges made absolutely no mention of his whistle-blowing or the press conference he had held for Berezovsky, but rather, accused him of "exceeding his official power and causing harm to witnesses," something his lawyers, provided by the state, told him involved the in-custody beating of a man who had been smuggling canned goods. Every journalist in the city seemed to be here at the trial that would either lead to his release or to another seeming lifetime in the soul-crushing prison. It was a frenzied feeding of the third estate.

Lefortovo had been a nightmare. Litvinenko's first lesson on the relativity of time, it was the longest eight months of his life. Separated from his wife and child, trapped in a cell next to murderers, traitors, thieves, and degenerates, he was horribly alone. Within that hell, he'd also experienced the longest minutes of his life—beatings he had received from prison guards for reasons unexplained. Then he had been placed in solitary confinement, locked in a cage barely wider than his shoulders, for infractions that he'd supposedly committed but that also were never made clear.

Most of it felt a blur, now, as he waited in that courtroom, expecting little but praying for justice from a judge he didn't know. His krysha, Berezovsky, had done his best, working behind the scenes to try to secure his release—but even Berezovsky's power seemed to have its limits. The new head of the FSB, Putin, had deemed Litvinenko a betrayer and traitor for turning on his agency. To Putin, the corruption that Litvinenko had revealed was less important than the disloyalty he had exhibited. Berezovsky had told him on one of his visits to Lefortovo that they should have foreseen the young FSB director's opinion on the matter; the reason Putin had been brought to Moscow from St. Petersburg in the first place was his steadfast belief in loyalty.

Berezovsky would do what he could, but Litvinenko also knew that the mogul was currently embroiled in his own drama—of a political nature. In business, the Oligarch was flying high, his fingers in oil, television, and now aluminum. But another election was looming, and this time there would be no propping up President Yeltsin. Even without the constitutional term limits that kept the president from running again, the man's health had deteriorated to the point that he was nearly a cadaver. After his latest heart attack—at least his fifth—the poor man now rarely appeared in public. Berezovsky and the Family were desperately searching for a replacement to run in Yeltsin's place—someone who would carry on the legacy that they, and Yeltsin, had created.

Compared to such important matters—the drama on the national stage—Litvinenko was merely a minor player, a bit part, a member of the chorus. The only person who truly thought of him as anything more was his ballroom dancer—who even now watched and waited with him from across the courtroom, her hands clasped together on her lap, helping him count down through those long, painful last few minutes.

Finally, there was a commotion from the front of the courtroom, caused by the judge's entrance. He strolled purposefully to his bench and reached for his gavel. He cleared his throat, adding agonizing seconds to the wait for his verdict—a new lesson for Litvinenko in the relativity of time.

Then, suddenly, he spat out, "Innocent of all charges."

Litvinenko's entire body stiffened as he digested what he had just heard. The courtroom erupted behind him, cameras flashing, and he could hear Marina laughing out loud with joy. One of the court bailiffs came over to unlock the docket where he was held and help Litvinenko out of his handcuffs. Litvinenko raised himself carefully to his feet and was about to take a step toward his wife, when suddenly there was a new commotion, an immense crash from the back of the long room. Litvinenko turned to see a dozen armed men burst into the courtroom. Garbed in camouflage uniforms, faces covered in black balaclavas, the men shoved the reporters aside as they moved down the center aisle, commanding the court bailiffs to stand aside. When they reached Litvinenko, two of them shouldered their automatic rifles, then grabbed him, yanking his arms back behind his back, clinking new cuffs around his wrists. Then they dragged him forward.

"You're under arrest," one of the men coughed in his ear.

"But the judge," Litvinenko stammered back, "he just said I'm innocent."

The man didn't respond. Litvinenko couldn't believe this was happening, right in front of all the news cameras. A judge had freed him, and now he was being rearrested right in the courtroom.

A message was clearly being sent. The armed men dragged him forward, roughly moving him past the reporters, who scrambled to get out of the way. As he passed Marina, one of the camouflaged men shoved him hard, and he could hear her gasp, shouting something, but then he was being dragged to the back door, toward the waiting unmarked cars outside.

Back to prison—and another lesson in the relativity of time.

CHAPTER EIGHTEEN

Fall 1999,

The Kremlin

BEREZOVSKY FELT HIS OWN heart dance to the staccato rhythm of Tatiana Yeltsin's heels against the polished marble of the floors as he followed her down the impossibly long hallway. He couldn't help but revel in the lowered eyes of the various pedestrian officials, security guards, and even members of the State Duma as they passed. Even at his normally frantic pace, he was struggling to keep up with the young woman. She knew this place better than anyone—hell, she had essentially grown up in the Kremlin—and obviously she had long ago filed away her route through the awe-inspiring surroundings that still tugged at Berezovsky's senses, threatening to muddle the important thoughts he was trying to organize inside his head. It wasn't merely the décor—the glittering crystal chandeliers above, the gilded ornamentation on the walls, the lavish, blood-red carpeting that covered sections of the marble floor, the doors they passed, so baroquely ornate, leading to historic chambers and famous ballrooms. Nor was it even the idea of the place, the fact that it was surrounded by walls in some places ten feet thick, bricked in red, a triangular fortress at the very heart of the city of Moscow—at the very heart of his beloved Russia. In some ways it was the very air itself, loaded with the taste of power. Stalin, Lenin, Gorbachev had breathed this same air, felt this same marble beneath their feet.

Of course, the daughter of the president and the Oligarch who had helped keep the man in power were far from wide-eyed tourists. The Kremlin was no museum to either of them. But Berezovsky couldn't shake the feeling that every step he took toward the interior of this seat of Russian power was like a pen stroke.

He had been to the Kremlin many times before; in fact, he had often conducted business in various outposts throughout the complex, in empty offices, anterooms, even hallways. He tried to find every excuse he could to conduct his trade beneath these crystal chandeliers. As often as he could, he made his important phone calls from this place, simply to better impress whoever was on the other end of the line. He had long ago learned that the best way to end a meeting, no matter where it took place, was to pretend to take a call from the Kremlin.

But in this instance, he hadn't joined Tatiana at the Kremlin for trumped-up reasons or to impress anyone. Just as in 1996, when he and his financier colleagues had faced an existential dilemma—the possibility of the Russian government falling back into Communist hands—they were once again at a crossroads.

In 1996, Berezovsky had been able to call together the Oligarchs, who were able to work together to essentially buy themselves a government. With Tatiana's help, they had been able to steer Yeltsin's inner circle away from the threats of Korzhakov and his hardliners—saving the democracy, keeping Yeltsin in place.

But this time around, no amount of money or maneuvering was going to give Yeltsin another term in the Kremlin. The constitutional term limits were clear, and his time at the helm was over. And even if they managed to construct a new constitution—something that had certainly been considered, but ruled out—the man simply wasn't strong enough or healthy enough to remain in power.

Just as in 1996, it was a dangerous moment for Russia and for Berezovsky, personally. He knew exactly how quickly things could change; and he also knew there were real limitations to his own power. Litvinenko's imprisonment was a clear indication of how even the smallest miscalculation on his part could lead to disaster.

Berezovsky blamed himself for the debacle with the young agent. Litvinenko's willingness to go public with his accusations against the FSB had saved Berezovsky from being a target for assassination, but it had also goaded the young new head of the FSB into making a show of force. Putin obviously saw Litvinenko as a traitor to the agency, his actions a betrayal to their code. Even so, firing the whistle-blower should have been enough. Having him arrested, sent to prison, and then rearrested after he served eight months, much of it in solitary confinement, seemed extreme. The dramatic scene—men in masks with submachine guns dragging him right out of the courtroom—was something directly out of the old KGB playbook.

Thankfully, Berezovsky had been able to sort out the situation, personally appealing to Vladimir Putin on Litvinenko's behalf. After a little back-and-forth, the agency had reluctantly released Litvinenko—though they had confiscated his passport and demanded that he remain in Moscow. Perhaps they really didn't know about the second set of identifications that he'd used in his days as an agent working undercover in Chechnya—or maybe they thought a warning would be enough to scare him into staying put. In any event, there was no doubt in Berezovsky's mind that Litvinenko couldn't remain in Russia any longer. The Oligarch had already begun making financial arrangements to help the young agent when he eventually resurfaced overseas, most likely in the UK, a country that went to considerable lengths to keep exiled asylum seekers safe.

But Berezovsky also felt that the dramatic episode had had a rather interesting silver lining. Advocating for the young agent had put Berezovsky in repeated contact with Vladimir Putin, and he had used the exchanges as an excuse to begin socializing with the FSB head. Over the days since Litvinenko's release, Berezovsky and Putin had become close. They had traveled together, dined together, and Putin had even been one of the many guests at Berezovsky's most recent birthday party, a lavish affair at the Logovaz Club.

Berezovsky found Putin surprisingly bright, even though he said little. He was conservative, to a fault, and held some level of fascination and nostalgia for the strong institutions of the old world—but he was also a true believer in the current democratic state, and the capitalistic forces that had opened up Russia since Yeltsin had taken power. Berezovsky found himself quite entranced by Putin, as he had become with Roman Abramovich, and had genuinely begun to consider him a friend. Even so, in political terms, he would most likely have still described the man as a useful cog, someone who could be trusted to behave loyally and without guile.

Still, Berezovsky had been somewhat surprised by his first inklings that the Family—most notably Tatiana, and through her, the president himself—had taken a real interest in Vladimir Putin, had even begun to consider him a potential heir to the Kremlin. His surprise had initially led him to resist the idea—not simply because of the Litvinenko affair, which was upsetting but, ultimately, something he could understand—but because he could think of other candidates who would be more malleable and perhaps more electable. But when he had sensed the wind behind Putin blowing stronger, the resolve of the Family growing, he realized that it would be in his own interests to get involved in the succession plan early. If he wanted to remain an important player in the next government, he needed to take a leading role in the efforts to plan and strategize Putin's ascension to the Kremlin. The election of 2000 needed to end, in many ways, as it had in 1996—with a debt owed to Boris Berezovsky.

Settling on one agreed-upon candidate was an important start. The revolving door of prime ministers that Yeltsin had subjected the country to had led to numerous dangerous moments for Berezovsky personally. In fact, one of the prime ministers, Yevgeny Primokov, also a former head of the intelligence division of the KGB, had taken direct aim at the Oligarch himself, along with his attorney general, Yuri Skuratov, perhaps because they believed Berezovsky wielded too much influence on Yeltsin's inner circle. Skuratov had initialized an investigation into Berezovsky's finances, eventually authorizing raids on Berezovsky's office—accusing him of stealing from Aeroflot and smuggling profits earned from the airline out of the country. When the masked federal agents had shown up, looking for incriminating documents, Berezovsky had been forced momentarily to flee to one of his châteaus in France. But he had quickly struck back—and in a particularly modern fashion. He had instructed ORT to air a video of a naked man—"a man who appeared to be Yuri Skuratov"—in bed with a pair of prostitutes. Shortly after the video aired, Skuratov was sacked—along with his prime minister—although Skuratov denied the allegations. Berezovsky had returned to Moscow in triumph—and then had used the momentum of the incident to get himself elected to the State Duma—an act which essentially made him immune to further criminal prosecution.

Berezovsky himself did not eventually appoint Putin to the

post of prime minister—but it was Berezovsky who had begun generating a fairly large bankroll, putting in place the means for the upcoming presidential campaign. He once again called on his colleagues, rivals, and especially the people he considered under his patronage—most notably Roman Abramovich, whose oil and aluminum interests generated the sort of cash flow necessary to elect yet another president.

But even with a considerable war chest, Putin was going to be a hard sell. Yeltsin's opponents had raised an interesting candidate in Yuri Luzhkov, the mayor of Moscow, who also happened to be Gusinsky's supporter and krysha. This meant that Berezovsky's main rival—and the owner of both NTV and Most Bank—was now firmly on the wrong side of the campaign. And further bad news: Luzhkov had a large following, and more important, he was the head of the popular All-Russia Party, which meant he would be guaranteed a large number—if not a definite majority—of votes.

As forward-thinking as Yeltsin's government had been—liberating the economy from the state through privatization and building a democracy—the one thing they had not constructed was an official party.

And that was exactly where Berezovsky had stepped in—and why Tatiana had summoned him behind the redbrick walls of the Kremlin. When Berezovsky had first presented her with his idea— really a stroke of brilliance—she had thought he was making a joke. But, as he laid the framework out for her, she began to realize that it really was an excellent strategy to build a base for Yeltsin's replacement, even before the campaign cycle began.

"The Unity Party," she mused, as she continued barreling down the long hallway. "It certainly has a nice ring to it."

Badri and Berezovsky had kicked the name around for quite

some time, before it had stuck. Out of thin air, a party to compete with All-Russia, built around one simple platform—unifying the country. Other than that, there were no specific party goals, although it had turned out that all the governors Yeltsin and the Family had convinced to join happened to support the ongoing War in Chechnya—which, in recent months, had taken a more serious turn.

That war support would infuse an immediate popularity to Unity—at the moment, the people of Russia were strongly in favor of dealing with the Chechens in as brutal a fashion as possible. A string of vicious terrorist bombings had hit apartment buildings all over the country—including Moscow itself. Blamed on Chechen separatists, these bombings had put the country on the offensive, and newly installed Prime Minister Putin had dealt with the situation with strength and determination that had won him many admirers. Relaunching the war with renewed vigor, he had given a nationally televised press conference—which Berezovsky had made sure was replayed on ORT over and over again—giving a rousing, steely-eyed speech: "We will annihilate them. We will chase them in the airports, even if they are on the toilet, we will go there and blow them up. Then this will be finished and done with."

But, even as Putin's popularity rose, he had been reluctant when faced with the idea of actually running for president; Berezovsky himself had spent time trying to convince the ex-KGB agent that he was needed, to save what they had built. Even so, it wasn't until Yeltsin himself pleaded with him, explaining that he was their best hope, that he finally acquiesced. Yeltsin understood that Putin had shown himself to be exactly the sort of strong-willed man of the people who the Russian populace loved. It was exactly that sort of strength that could carry the new Unity Party, which was designed to put him in power.

"A party, financing, and my media," Berezovsky responded, breathing quickly as he worked to keep up with the redheaded vortex of motion next to him. "Will it be enough?"

"And your own limitless energy," Tatiana added. "Don't forget your limitless energy, Boris. A man who dreams up parties out of thin air."

"If having energy is my main crime, I will be remembered well—when this is eventually written about in the history books."

Tatiana smiled.

"It will only be written about if we win. A brand-new party isn't going to be able to grow fast enough in a year to compete with All-Russia. The mayor has important friends, too, and NTV will be on his side. The people will see him as an alternative, maybe even a move toward a strength and stability that we've been lacking. Russian people love strength."

Putin's jump in the popularity polls after his decisive handling of the Chechen situation was proof. Not diplomacy, not words, but precise, definite action—that's what the Russian people wanted. That's what they fell for. But for Putin to sustain that for the entire campaign that was ahead of them—it would be a herculean task.

"What if there was a way," Tatiana suddenly asked, thinking along the same lines, "of accelerating the situation? Of pushing the opposition back on its heels?"

Berezovsky raised an eyebrow, looking at her.

"What do you mean?"

The year 2000 isn't simply a new beginning because of the election, she explained. It was the beginning of a new millennium. The whole world was preparing for the biggest celebration in recent history, for a brand-new century, to begin on midnight, New Year's Eve.

"My father's term ends next June," she continued, "but the moment of rebirth will not wait until June. The millennium begins in three months."

Berezovsky began to understand what she was saying—and he felt that familiar electricity rising in his bones.

If she was really saying what he believed she was saying, if she was proposing a plan of action around the sentiment—it would be like an earthquake. It would take the country by surprise, knock the opposition not just back on their heels, but right out of the race.

Berezovsky's Unity Party was a stroke of genius, but what Tatiana was proposing—what she could no doubt achieve if she were able to convince her father to take one giant step—would be momentous.

"Ideas like this change history," Berezovsky mused.

Tatiana looked at him, though she never stopped moving forward.

"You're wrong about that. Ideas float around, like the breeze swirling beneath the spruce trees that line Red Square. Ideas are little more than air. Men and women change history."

Berezovsky smiled.

"And sometimes we do it even before history realizes it's time to change."

CHAPTER NINETEEN

December 31, 1999, 11:58 a.m.,
Logovaz Club

E VEN THOUGH BEREZOVSKY HAD suspected that something
unusual was going to happen before the end of the year, when the
moment finally came, sudden and without warning—it hit him like
a hammer, as it had been designed to do. One minute he was sitting
next to Badri in the club, chatting about various nonsense, glancing
occasionally at the large-screen television on the wall—and then the
screen suddenly froze and went black. Then bright, breaking-news
banners appeared, casting red reflections off the Logovaz walls.

Boris Yeltsin's face appeared on the screen, his skin a winter
night's shade of gray, his eyes sunken and tired, but still sparkling
from an energy somewhere deep inside, still hinting at the charisma
that had raised him so far and kept him in power for so long. Yeltsin
remained silent for a moment, staring into the camera, as the audience took in the background of his roost in the Kremlin, the large
holiday tree behind, flanked by the flags of his office. The president
began to speak.

Dear Russians!

A very short time remains before a magical date in our history. The year 2000 is approaching. A new century, a new millennium.

We have all pondered this date. We have pondered, beginning in childhood, then having grown up, how old we would be in 2000, and how old our mothers would be, and how old our children would be. At some point, this unusual New Year seemed so far away. Now this day is upon us.

Dear friends! My dear ones!

Today I am turning to you for the last time with New Year's greetings. But that's not all. Today I am turning to you for the last time as president of Russia.

I have made a decision.

I thought long and hard over it. Today, on the last day of the departing century, I am resigning.

I have heard many times that "Yeltsin will hang onto power by any means, he won't give it to anyone." That's a lie.

But that's not the point. I have always said that I would not depart one bit from the Constitution. That parliamentary elections should take place in the constitutionally established terms. That was done. And I also wanted presidential elections to take place on time—in June 2000. This was very important for Russia. We are creating a very important precedent of a civilized, voluntary transfer of power, power from one president of Russia to another, newly elected one.

And still, I made a different decision. I am leaving. I am leaving earlier than the set term.

I have understood that it was necessary for me to do this. Russia must enter the new millennium with new politicians, with new faces, with new, smart, strong, energetic people.

And we who have been in power for many years already, we must go.

Seeing with what hope and faith people voted in the parliamentary elections for a new generation of politicians, I understood that I have completed the main thing of my life. Already, Russia will never return to the past. Now, Russia will always move only forward.

And I should not interfere with this natural march of history. To hold onto power for another half-year, when the country has a strong man who is worthy of being president and with whom practically every Russian today ties his hopes for the future? Why should I interfere with him? Why wait still another half-year? No, that's not for me. It's simply not in my character.

Today, on this day that is so extraordinarily important for me, I want to say just a few more personal words than usual.

I want to ask for your forgiveness.

For the fact that many of the dreams we shared did not come true. And for the fact that what seemed simple to us turned out to be tormentingly difficult. I ask forgiveness for not justifying some hopes of those people who believed that at one stroke, in one spurt, we could leap from the gray, stagnant, totalitarian past into the light, rich, civilized future. I myself believed in this, that we could overcome everything in one spurt.

I turned out to be too naive in something. In some places, problems seemed to be too complicated. We forced our way forward through mistakes, through failures. Many people in this hard time experienced shock.

But I want you to know. I have never said this. Today it's important for me to tell you. The pain of each of you has called forth pain in me, in my heart. Sleepless nights, tormenting worries—

about what needed to be done, so that people could live more easily and better. I did not have any more important task.

I am leaving. I did all I could—not according to my health, but on the basis of all the problems. A new generation is relieving me, a generation of those who can do more and better.

In accordance with the Constitution, as I resign, I have signed a decree placing the duties of the president of Russia on the head of government, Vladimir Vladimirovich Putin. For three months, again in accordance with the Constitution, he will be the head of state. And in three months, presidential elections will take place.

I have always been certain of the surprising wisdom of Russians. That's why I don't doubt what choice you will make at the end of March 2000.

Bidding farewell, I want to tell each of you: Be happy. You deserve happiness. You deserve happiness and calm.

Happy New Year! Happy new century, my dear ones![*]

As Yeltsin finished with his resignation speech, Berezovsky managed to tear his eyes from the television screen. There were more than a handful of men and women in the club at that time—the middle of the day, on the eve of the new millennium—and yet every one of them seemed rooted to the floor. The expressions on each face ranged from confusion to total shock. Not only was this event unexpected—it was entirely unheard of: a seated president, one who had held on to power through every means possible, resigning on New Year's Eve, six months before the presidential election. Handing over the presidency to his prime minister—Vladimir Putin, a man who

---

had really seemed to come from nowhere, a former KGB officer and recent head of the FSB, a prime minister who had thrilled the country by his use of force in Chechnya, but who otherwise had a fairly blank résumé, a shadow for a history.

Yeltsin's exit had come without warning. As he had said in his own resignation speech, the expectations had been for him to try to hold onto power no matter what the cost—eventually, the assumption was, he'd have to be dragged out of office by his hands and feet. After all, this was a man who had survived multiple coup attempts, multiple heart attacks, the fall of an economy, and two wars in Chechnya. And yet he had just handed the presidency over without a single shot fired.

"Our hippie writer has certainly outdone himself this time," Badri commented, when he'd found his voice. "That was a hell of a speech."

Whether Yumashev had written the words or Yeltsin had been involved in the writing himself, it really had been a perfect speech for the most shocking and brilliant turn of events. Putin had been riding high on his popularity as a strong, decisive prime minister— and now suddenly he was acting president. Yeltsin had said there would still be an election in three months—but in three months, with Putin running the country from a position of strength, with the new Unity Party behind him—hell, he would now be going into the elections as the front-runner, when yesterday he had been going in as a distant second.

"Winning by resigning," Berezovsky said. "I wouldn't have thought it was possible."

Tomorrow, Vladimir Putin would be sworn in as acting president. And then, with much fanfare, Vladimir Putin would take over as the new president of Russia.

And it was also clear—the young president would owe a debt

to Boris Berezovsky. This time, Berezovsky might not have bought and paid for the government, as in 1996—but this president still owed his ascendancy, in part, to the onetime car salesman and current Kremlin power broker.

Berezovsky exhaled, speaking mostly under his breath.

"But still, business as usual," he said, and he could see from the Georgian's face that his friend was hoping it was true.

Boris Yeltsin had made history. Vladimir Putin was now president. But for Boris Berezovsky, this was really about the business of Boris Berezovsky. And all indications pointed to the notion that, as usual, business was good.

CHAPTER TWENTY

June 15, 2000,

Alexandrovka Dacha

BEREZOVSKY'S WORLD HAD FLIPPED upside down many times over the past decade, so he shouldn't have been surprised when once again it spun out from beneath his feet. This time, though, it happened in the course of a mere six months—a lifetime in modern Russia, where it took no longer than a five-minute speech for an unknown man to become president.

Still, Berezovsky had found himself floundering when this new existential challenge blindsided him. Maybe it was fitting that this new threat came from the same nowhere man they had just installed as president. It wasn't just those in the outside world who had little information about Putin's past, before his days at the Kremlin. Berezovsky and the Family had been impressed by his service in the mayor's office of St. Petersburg, but much of his work at the KGB before that was barely documented. How well did any of them really know the man?

Even after the imprisonment of Litvinenko, Berezovsky had believed they had chosen someone who could be controlled from behind the scenes. But a few weeks before the official election, with Putin already ahead in the polls, the acting president suddenly revealed a side he hadn't shown before.

On March 26, he had called a television press conference and had spoken about the chaotic business environment gripping the country, and the role of businessmen going forward. Berezovsky had been sitting exactly where he was now, at his breakfast table in his dacha, watching the conference before he headed to the Logovaz Club. Putin had looked impressive on the television screen—exactly as he had been designed to appear, young, handsome, brimming with confidence and strength, exactly the man depicted in all the feature stories they had played on ORT over the months of the campaign—often showing Putting in judo gear, riding horses, or swimming. A very different leader from the aging, sick Yeltsin, Putin was a symbol of the new generation, of youth. And then he began to speak.

"Those who combine power and capital—in the future, these Oligarchs will cease to exist as a class."

Berezovsky had been shocked by the sweep and ferocity of the statement. As different news programs analyzed the conference, the consensus was that Putin was calling for the elimination of Berezovsky and his colleagues as a power bloc. These were frightening words—and to Berezovsky, who had been funding Putin's rise in the polls, they'd come out of nowhere.

As he'd watched the fallout on TV, he'd realized that Putin's statement only made the president more popular. The public, most of whom lived at or near poverty, had grown increasingly frustrated watching men like Berezovsky living like royalty, right in their midst. The people didn't know, or care, that Berezovsky and his colleagues believed they had saved capitalism and democracy from the communists. In Berezovsky's view, the Oligarchs had benefited only because they had been smart enough and quick enough to do so. Yet all the people cared about was that Putin was now presenting himself as the man who would clean up the chaos and drive the Oligarchs out of politics.

It was as if the man had awakened one morning with a brand-new morality, intending to clean up the business world that had propped him up, that had invented the very party he was leading. He was suddenly hungry for the hand that fed him.

And it hadn't ended there. Putin easily won the election, and his inauguration was an event befitting a new kind of royalty, conducted with all the pomp and circumstance of the Kremlin of old. Putin regally strode down an extensive red carpet to take his seat, applauded from all sides by his supporters. Shortly thereafter, he had summoned all of the Oligarchs to appear at the Kremlin right next to him, in front of the cameras, and had given another speech explaining that, from that moment on, there would be a separation of business and politics—that businessmen were to pay their taxes and run their companies, while he would run the government. No more just a matter of campaign, no more simply pandering to popular sentiment—this was going to be policy.

Words were words. Berezovsky was a master of words, and he knew they were only as strong as the intent of the men who spoke them. But any hope that Putin had just been posturing for the cameras was dashed, as Berezovsky watched the new breaking report that was now being replayed over and over again on his own ORT. In a different time, at an earlier moment in his life, the same report would have thrilled him to the core. But now, what was unfolding in front of him stirred an apocalyptic fear in his soul.

The episode itself had begun a few days earlier, when Putin had decided to follow his harsh words against the "Oligarchs as a class" by putting the squeeze on one of the most well-known and powerful of them all, Vladimir Gusinsky, who also happened to have supported his competitor in the election, the mayor of Moscow. Gusinsky, Berezovsky's former enemy, had also helped keep Yeltsin in power—had been using his resources at Most Bank and his NTV network to push against Putin both before and after the election. Now Putin had struck back. A government investigation into Gusinsky had discovered that state money had been illegally moving from Gazprom, the gas giant, into Gusinsky's television and media network in the form of loans that weren't being paid back, and that there had also been episodes of tax evasion and corrupt enrichment. Gusinsky had immediately lashed back, angrily calling Putin a war criminal for the campaign in Chechnya. Gusinsky was promptly arrested, although he maintains his innocence.

During his short stay in prison, Gusinsky had apparently been given a choice: face criminal charges that could keep him locked up for years or sell his shares in Media-Most, NTV, and much of his other businesses—many of which were on the verge of bankruptcy—to Gazprom. If he went through with the sale, essentially divesting himself from Russian business, he would be allowed to leave prison, and the country.

Gusinsky had taken the offer. Upon his release a few days later, he sold NTV and his bank, took his remaining billions, and immediately fled to Spain.

Once upon a time, Berezovsky had celebrated when his rival had been forced out of the country. But this time, it was different. This was not temporary as it had been years before. Gusinsky wouldn't be coming back. One of the biggest and most powerful Oligarchs alive, a man worth billions, he would now live in exile. If he were ever to return, he would face criminal charges and, most likely, prison.

Listening to the journalists analyze the situation, Berezovsky grew angrier. There was now no doubt: Putin intended to go after them all, one by one. Roman Abramovich, and probably Badri, would have cautioned him to stay quiet, under the radar. Putin wasn't yet gunning for him personally, and Sibneft and Abramovich's aluminum concerns were still bringing in barrels of money—from which Berezovsky was receiving his weekly payments.

But Berezovsky simply wasn't built that way—he couldn't sit still, he couldn't be silent. Such behavior was not in his nature. The way he saw it, he had faced many battles before. Why should he view Putin as anything more than another obstacle in his path? He had survived multiple assassination attempts, a near prosecution over Aeroflot, the battle with Korzhakov. He could survive Vladimir Putin.

Of course, in the past he had always had somewhere to turn, a krysha in the Kremlin with enough power to protect him, to set things right. But now the Family was gone. Tatiana still worked as Yeltsin's personal assistant without pay, but she didn't have any real power, and would soon be leaving the Kremlin for good. Yeltsin had retired and vanished into the country. On the political front, Berezovsky had few allies and no power base.

But that didn't mean the Oligarch was without weapons. He had his own money, he had Abramovich's continuing asset stream, and, most important of all, he had a television network.

All he really needed was for Putin to give him an opening and he would strike, quick and venomous, and show the young president that it would be better to negotiate than to fight an all-out war.

Berezovsky's hands balled into fists against the breakfast table. At the motion, he inadvertently touched the edge of the envelope that had been delivered the morning before, which he'd opened but left right where he had first read the contents. It was an invitation—

not addressed to Berezovsky, but to one of his business associates, another of the Oligarchs. The official, embossed calligraphy on the invitation itself was as ornate as Putin's inauguration ceremony had been; but the words—and the terrifying address, where a group of his best-known Oligarch colleagues had been invited, to attend an afternoon tea—were something out of the distant past.

Despite his anger and frustration at how quickly his world had changed, Berezovksy had to applaud Putin's flair for the dramatic. An invitation to tea, asking the Oligarchs—as a class—to gather together in a place they all knew well—Stalin's Moscow home, as famous for the leader's purges as it was for various meetings of great political importance—it was a message that the Oligarchs would receive loud and clear. Putin's work wasn't finished; Gusinsky had been a warning shot, and they would do well to pay attention.

Berezovksy slammed his hand down on the invite—then crumpled it into a ball and threw it toward a wastebasket in the corner of his breakfast room. He himself hadn't yet received an invitation to the tea, but if he did, he would ignore the summons. He would go out on his yacht in the Caribbean or vacation at his home in the South of France. Let the other Oligarchs remain silent, let the others bow down to the new czar. Berezovksy wasn't going to stand by and listen to another lecture on business in modern Russia. *He had invented business in modern Russia.* Instead, he would enjoy himself and his wealth, all the while waiting, like a coiled snake, for Vladimir Putin to make a mistake, to misstep in any way.

And when it happened, Berezovsky would be ready. He would strike back, and Putin would realize who he was really dealing with.

CHAPTER TWENTY-ONE

August 12, 2000,

11:30 a.m., Barents Sea

BENEATH THE SEA IN a nuclear submarine is a setting that few people in the world will experience; but for Lieutenant Captain Dmitri Kolesnikov, it was as natural and familiar as his childhood home in St. Petersburg, or the apartment he shared with his wife of three months, or the naval training camps where he had spent much of his young life.

Kolesnikov was crouched low in the cramped Seventh Compartment of the Oscar Class nuclear submarine—a 943-model attack vessel capable of carrying dozens of nuclear-tipped cruise missiles, a battery of torpedoes, a dozen mines, a slew of antiaircraft mortars. Hell, it was one of the largest submarines ever built, over five hundred feet long, one of only five in the Northern Fleet. Bathed in the harsh, fluorescent light reflecting off the thick steel walls and iron-plated floors, he worked his way between the various hissing pipes and clicking knobs of his turbine station.

The vessel was still at periscope depth—right below the surface of the churning, frozen waters of this area of the Barents Sea, near the desolate northwestern coast of Russia—and he could feel the slight rocking of the current, something that might have bothered the stomach and the inner ear of a less-experienced sailor but barely registered with him.

To say that Dmitri had been born a submariner would not have been an exaggeration; he had followed his father's footsteps into the navy, and into the company of men who lived much of their lives beneath the surface. His proudest achievement was the day he had gained command of this Seventh Compartment, making him an integral part of his crew of one hundred eighteen officers and enlisted men. They were brothers, all, who had chosen a way of life defined by the close, unique environment inside that submerged steel tube.

Dmitri worked diligently and efficiently at his station, as orders filtered through the intercom system above his head from the command compartment, four sections ahead along the chassis of the narrow vessel. Even though this was only a training mission, his crew was taking part in a series of naval games being conducted by the Northern Fleet, and he took his duties seriously. The truth was, every moment aboard a nuclear submarine had to be taken seriously. Every submariner knew there were no margins for error, that the only thing that separated them from certain death was a hull made of steel, titanium, and iron and the diligence of the brothers who also wore the uniform.

The brotherhood was so thick Dmitri could taste it in the air they all shared. A hundred and eighteen men breathing the same recycled oxygen, bathing in and drinking from the same recycled water. An almost organic system, unlike any in the outside world. The significance of every moment was made more real by the fact that there was no sense of night or day, no windows. The fluorescent light, a constant glow, penetrated Dmitri's thoughts even when he slept on that steel shell of a bunk he called his own, in a room near the front of the sub, crowded together with brothers for months at a time.

It didn't matter that the two torpedoes his vessel was about to fire at the nearby battle cruiser—the *Pyotr Velikiy*—were actually dummy weapons, little more than fueled metal pipes that would do no more damage to the hull of the ship than a rock from a slingshot. For the men aboard the *Kursk*, the mission was as real as life and death.

Approximately a minute later, when the order to fire reverberated through the intercom, Dmitri felt the vessel tremble beneath his feet. His finely trained ears could hear the whisper of the torpedoes leaving the tubes, followed by the rush of water as they tore toward their target. Dmitri allowed himself a smile as he continued checking his turbine controls. The sheer power of his vessel never ceased to amaze him, releasing a kind of primal energy inside his own veins.

His mind was still picturing those twin mock torpedoes spiraling through the deep cold water a second later, when suddenly, there was a terrifying noise, a blast so loud that spikes of pain tore through his eardrums. The submarine—his entire world—lunged upward. Dimitri toppled forward, slamming into the hard metal floor chin first and for a brief second his vision blurred. Then his adrenaline spiked, his training kicked in, and his eyes opened.

Everything around him seemed to slow, as the chaotic moment unfolded. He could feel a surge of the sub's engines, as someone in the command center tried desperately to raise the ship. And then, just as suddenly, they were diving, but not in any controlled fashion, not in any manner he had experienced before in the smooth descent of the most sophisticated war machine of the Russian nation. This was a desperate, horrifying plunge. Dimitri flung out both hands, grabbing hold of one of the nearest steam pipes in an attempt to hold himself upright—and then the entire submarine somersaulted, flipping him up into the air, then sending him crashing back down again. The fluorescent lights flickered, but somehow held; even so, all he could see was pure mayhem, a blur of equipment flying through the air, other crewmen crashing into the ceiling and the walls and the floor. The air filled with screams and the horrible screeching of rending metal. Even worse, Dimitri could hear the thunder of water rushing into the vessel—but thankfully, not yet into his own compartment.

His terror was intense, paralyzing, but Dimitri refused to give in. He concentrated on counting out the seconds as they descended, calculating depth. He had reached about three hundred and fifty feet when there was another ferocious crash, and his body was slammed upward—the sub careening at full descent into the ocean floor. Barely a second later, there were multiple explosions in rapid succession and the sickening feeling of part of the hull ahead tearing apart.

More frantic screams and then crewmen pushed past Dmitri, rushing toward the rear compartment. Without thinking, Dmitri let his own reflexes take over, and he followed them through the vessel, shouting for others to follow, grabbing a bleeding, wounded sailor by the arm, dragging him along. *Go, go, go!* They raced from his turbine compartment, Seven, into Eight, and then through that into the rear and final cabin, Nine. There was an escape hatch in the back of the ninth compartment, along with enough rescue, pressure-protective suits to keep them alive, even at such a depth. He had no idea what had happened, whether they had collided with something under the water, hit an errant mine or an enemy torpedo, or whether one of the dummies had simply malfunctioned and sent them to the floor. But he was fairly certain that, once they had hit the bottom, the force had detonated their payload of real torpedoes. He could only be thankful that the sub wasn't carrying any nuclear-tipped armament during the training session. But he had no doubt that the submarine was damaged beyond repair. From the force of the explosions he had felt, and from the way the vessel had somersaulted on its way down to the ocean floor, he believed that the front half of the *Kursk* had been destroyed, perhaps all the way back through the command center, to the engines themselves.

Which meant they had very little time before power was gone, and along with it, the breathable air they had left.

He leapt forward into the rear compartment, and went to work with the other seamen, sealing off the cabin. Then he glanced around the small confines and counted the remaining crew. *Twenty-three men.* The Seventh, Eighth, and Ninth compartments had a crew of twenty-four all together. It appeared that almost all of them had made it to the back of the vessel. But the rest of the sub's crew was gone. Listening at the door they were sealing, he could hear nothing behind it but creaking metal and the rush of water. He could only hope that the rest of his brothers had died instantly as the vessel had crashed into the ground.

After they had finished sealing off the door, he turned his attention to the rear of the Ninth Compartment, to the group of crewmen milling around the escape hatch. But as he looked at the focus of their work, his stomach dropped. Even from across the compartment, Dimitri could see that the hatch was warped inward at the center—the metal curling over itself, the release mechanisms melded together in a tangle of iron and steel. The damage was severe, and with the tools they had available in the rear compartment, it was doubtful they were ever going to get through.

Dimitri's legs grew heavy. The men near the escape hatch spoke in frantic, clipped words, but he already knew what the others were now realizing: their situation was hopeless. He let himself drop slowly to the floor, his back leaning upright against the sealed inner hatch behind him, his breathing slowing, his heart strangely calm in his chest.

In the weeks leading up to this mission, the twenty-seven-year-old had felt a sort of premonition. Normally optimistic and high-spirited, he had felt so strongly that something might soon go wrong that he had even given his young wife of only a few months a short poem about the fragility of life. The poem had ended quite simply, and quite sadly: *I want time to whisper one thing, my darling, I love you.*

At that moment, Dmitri didn't know how much time he had left to whisper anything. He guessed maybe a few hours of air, which he could already sense was rapidly filling with toxic levels of carbon dioxide, as well as peroxide, most likely from the destroyed torpedoes. Even though other boats nearby would have seen them go down, and a rescue effort would be waged, it was doubtful anyone would get to them in time.

A few hours left to whisper, but maybe he could do something more significant. He crawled across the compartment, and began searching the low desks and cabinets riveted to the nearby wall. He quickly found half of what he needed—a writing instrument, but no blank sheets of paper. He grabbed a nearby book and tore a number of pages free. Then he dropped back into a sitting position, his back against a free section of the wall, and began to write.

He started with a personal message to his wife. All the things he never had the time to tell her. And then he switched back to his official capacity—and dutifully noted what he had experienced, logging as much as he could for the rescue divers who would eventually find them. He noted the time, in military style: 15:45.

As he worked, the fluorescent lights dimmed: *It is dark to write, but I will try, I feel it seems we have no chance, I hope someone will find this . . .*

After that, he listed the twenty-three men who were in the compartment with him. And he continued writing, trying to continue as long as the air was still breathable: *There is no need for despair . . .*

Then the lights went out. Still, in complete blackness, trying his best to ignore the terrified voices around him, he continued, doing his best to feel the pencil against the paper, knowing that his handwriting had become a nearly indecipherable crawl. The air grew thicker, his vision began to swirl, but still he wrote, for as long as he could.

Before he finally lost consciousness, he found something plastic to wrap his note inside, then placed the package carefully in the pocket of his naval uniform.

The last thing he did, before he closed his eyes, was whisper, one last time.

CHAPTER TWENTY-TWO

Late August 2000,

Office of Alexander Voloshin, chief of the

Presidential Administration, the Kremlin

*P*USH AND PUSH AND *push, and sometimes a tree limb bends, some-times it breaks. Sometimes it does neither of these things, sometimes it snaps back at you, with deadly force . . .*

Berezovksy paced across the small anteroom outside of Alexander Voloshin's office like a caged animal, occasionally eyeing the heavy wooden door that led into the chief of staff's chambers, wondering what he would face when he was finally allowed inside. It all seemed so ironic, how not long ago being summoned behind the red walls of the Kremlin had been such an honor. Now it was like a lead pipe against the back of his knees. He knew exactly why he was there, why Voloshin had sent him the urgent "invitation." Berezovsky had forced his way to this moment from the very second that the first reports of the tragedy at the bottom of the Barents had become international news.

The story had rightly gripped the nation and the world. Even now, two weeks later, the country was reeling from the loss of the submariners and the dramatic, often conflicting details of the explosion, sinking, and failed rescue efforts that had been played out like a soap opera in the national press. It didn't matter that everyone knew that the young men were doomed; the suspense of knowing they were trapped at the bottom of the sea and then the need to recover their remains kept the tragic story front-page news for weeks.

To Berezovsky, the event was more than a national catastrophe. It was an opportunity, an opening: the government was helpless to save the one hundred and eighteen men in the submarine, and the longer the salvage operation took, the worse the situation looked. Berezovsky had seized on the story as the perfect vehicle to go after Putin. There was nothing a man like Putin hated more than the feeling of impotence. And with the entire world watching, there was little Putin could do that would look effective. In fact, when the incident had first occurred, the president had been in the midst of a vacation in the summer resort at Sochi. Instead of rushing to the scene, and in his view causing more chaos, he had decided to remain in Sochi and coordinate the government oversight of the rescue attempts from there.

Berezovsky had jumped on this decision as a sign of the president's inaccessibility and weakness in the face of a tragedy. He had personally stepped in and pushed ORT to go relentlessly negative—attacking and criticizing the president at every turn. When confusing reports came out from the Russian Navy about what had caused the explosion—whether it had been an enemy torpedo or an accident—and whether or not there had been any survivors somehow clinging to life after the explosions had sunk the sub—ORT had put the blame squarely on Putin.

For a time, Berezovsky's machinations had seemed to be working. Using the distraught families of the *Kursk* sailors as fodder, he had launched volley after volley at the navy and the president. Televised protests and memorials led to critical newspaper articles, which led to even more protests.

As Berezovsky had predicted, Putin had taken the criticism personally. Perhaps *too* personally. On August 22, the president had spoken to journalists and had specifically targeted Berezovsky in his response to those who had attacked him in the press: "They are liars. The television people who have been destroying the state for ten years, they have been stealing money and buying up absolutely everything, now they are trying to discredit the country so that the army ends up even worse."

Two days later, in the *Financial Times*, Putin went on the attack again, singling out "Oligarchs who have given money to the crew's families"—a direct reference to Boris Berezovsky, the *Times* pointed out, because one of Berezovsky's newspapers had run a charity drive aimed at providing aid to the victims' kin—"who would have done better to sell their villas on the Mediterranean, on the coasts of France and Spain—and maybe then they could explain why the property was registered under false names and behind legal firms, and we should probably ask the question—where is it this money came from?"

Berezovsky was stung by those words and realized that his campaign against Putin had perhaps been going a little too well. Putin's veiled threat—changing the conversation from the sinking of the *Kursk* to looking into the finances of a certain Oligarch—immediately brought up thoughts of Gusinsky, now in exile. Berezovsky realized he had pushed the president into focusing on him personally, a dangerous situation.

Then came the summons, barely a day after Putin's frightening words, demanding that Berezovsky come to the Kremlin to talk.

Now, pacing outside Voloshin's office, Berezovsky's insides were engaged in a battle between fear and anger; he wasn't used to waiting, and a man of his status shouldn't have been terrified to sit down with a presidential administrator. This was *Berezovsky's* Kremlin. And this was supposed to be *Berezovsky's* president. Certainly, he had forced Putin's hand, he had poked at the president until the man had to respond. He should have been aware of the ramifications of steering ORT in that direction, but the way he saw it, he hadn't had a choice. Putin had brought this down on himself.

When the door finally opened, and Voloshin stepped out to officiously usher Berezovsky inside, the Oligarch's emotions were almost at a volcanic level. He could barely hear the presidential administrator's short welcome through the rush of blood in his ears. He marched past the taller man, ignoring the look of concern that spread across the administrator's bearded face, and into the office, where his attention was immediately drawn to the second man, seated behind Voloshin's desk.

It almost took him a moment to recognize the president, the young man had changed so much since he'd taken office. Berezovsky felt he was looking at something he and Badri had dreamed up for a campaign poster. Immaculate, tailored blue suit, stiff, strong shoulders, a scowl across his youthful, confident face. Putin had much more presence than volume, and he projected a power that seemed to suck all the air out of the room. This was not the same obsequious, attentive young man Berezovsky had dined with, traveled with, and had even needed to convince to take the mantle of leadership from Yeltsin. This was no longer the reluctant heir. This man was born to wield power. And at the moment, his expression was both dismissive and angry. Even so, unlike Berezovsky, he was in control of his features and emotions. He was in control of everything. After a lifetime in the KGB, a childhood filled with judo training and street fighting, he exuded inner strength.

Berezovsky realized that he had miscalculated again. First, he had put his money, talent, and media behind Putin, helping to put him in the Kremlin. Now he was facing off with a force of nature in a battle that he might already have lost.

The door slammed shut behind Berezovsky, and Voloshin began to talk, his words rapid and clipped. Berezovsky kept his eyes on Putin, barely hearing what Voloshin was saying. The Oligarch's emotions were so high, he would never be sure that how he remembered the scene had much to do with what had actually transpired or if it was a mingling of the conversation in the room, and the subtext of threats and accusations he believed were beneath the actual words. In the end, whatever the presidential administrator said, the real power was with the man behind the desk.

Somewhere within his monologue, Voloshin reached the point of the summons and made an accusation that Berezovksy certainly couldn't refute: Berezovsky had been using the television station ORT as his own personal megaphone. Despite the fact that he and his partners only controlled a forty-nine-percent stake in the network, Berezovsky had been controlling the content and programming, sticking his nose into the daily management of ORT for his own benefit. Voloshin had it on good authority that Berezovsky had been leaning on the general director of the network several times a day, forcing the man to replay negative coverage of the *Kursk* situation; furthermore, Berezovsky had corralled the on-air journalists themselves, guiding them to focus on criticizing Putin's handling of the tragedy.

Through his anger, Berezovsky waved off Voloshin. It was a big news story, Berezovsky said, and ORT was simply covering the drama from every angle. The journalists were simply doing their jobs, and Berezovsky had a responsibility to the people of Russia to help his network report the news. Berezovsky didn't really care what Voloshin thought of his methods, he wanted to know where this was leading.

Eventually, Voloshin got to the point: "The government wants you to stop using ORT for your own benefit. You need to stop influencing management."

"What exactly does that mean?" Berezovsky demanded. "What are you getting at?"

His attention remained fixed on Putin, who was watching the interchange with narrowed eyes.

Voloshin continued in a calm but direct manner: "From here on out, you will no longer be involved in management of ORT with regard to content. It's as simple as that. As long as you are not in control, as long as you're not influencing the shows that are on the air, you will not be a problem to us, and no more formal steps will be needed."

Formal steps. Berezovsky had a good idea what Voloshin meant by that. Berezovsky tried to control himself, but he was already too far gone. After the fact, he couldn't be sure what was said, but he certainly raised his voice, his words rapid. In his opinion, this was an out-and-out threat. Even though he couldn't be sure whether or not Gusinsky's name had been used, he believed the implication was there: those *formal steps* could mean imprisonment, exile, or worse. Voloshin was asking him—no, was demanding—that he step back from his position at ORT and give up control of the network. Voloshin countered his angry storm with calmer statements of fact— that forty-nine percent did not make ORT his personal soapbox, that he couldn't put on the air whatever he wanted. But Berezovsky only heard the threats, not the logic: he only understood the subtext. Voloshin was telling him to back off, and Putin was nodding along, because, no doubt, this was coming from the president, not his functionary. *The same president who had recently spoken about ending the Oligarchs as a class.*

"This isn't right," Berezovsky heard himself fume. "On what authority can you make such a demand?"

Putin rose from behind the desk, and Berezovsky went silent. The air in the room was like a scarf pulled tight.

It has been decided, the words came again, either from Putin or Voloshin, though it didn't really matter. Berezovsky knew exactly who was drawing the line that he would have been a fool to try to cross. *It has been decided that you can no longer control ORT in this manner.*

The rest of the conversation was less clear and direct; after the fact, it was uncertain whether anyone had demanded that Berezovsky hand anything over to the state, or if Gusinsky's name had ever come up in that room. What was certain, what was clear, was that Berezovsky had to step back from ORT. It wasn't a matter for debate. Still, Berezovsky couldn't accept what he was being told, he refused to be ordered around like a dog. He heard himself respond angrily once again, saying something about the government wanting to control the media, to destroy private business, to turn the clock back to the tyrannical old days. But by then, Berezovsky was sputtering, nearly incomprehensible.

Eventually, he did calm himself down enough to understand that the meeting was over—there was nothing left for him to say. Voloshin shook Berezovsky's hand, signaling that it was time to leave. And then suddenly Putin crossed the room to Berezovsky as well.

"Good-bye," the president said, quietly. "Boris Abramovich."

Berezovsky stared at him. It was the first time Putin had ever addressed him using the formal form of his name, the formal patronymic. Up to that point, Putin had always called him Boris. This was almost certainly a signal, and not at all a pleasant one.

"Good-bye," Berezovsky responded, with a hint of actual sadness. "Volodya."

If Putin noticed Berezovsky's use of the familiar diminutive, he didn't show it. He simply gestured toward the door.

CHAPTER TWENTY-THREE

August 27, 2000,

Logovaz Club

THE PHONE WAS LIKE a lead weight against Badri Patarkatsish-vili's ear, as he immediately recognized the voice on the other end of the line. It wasn't the sort of phone call any Russian—or Georgian, for that matter—ever wanted to receive, and at that particular moment, the events Badri had been watching unfold on the television set hanging above his head only made the situation more terrifying.

Just an hour or two before, Badri had settled into his usual roost at the club to watch the country's newest tragedy unfold; both ORT and NTV had been replaying the bizarre footage over and over again, the dramatic report knocking the *Kursk* tragedy off of the screen—not because of anything Berezovsky or ORT's management had decreed—but because another real-world event had suddenly intruded on the internal political battle being played out around them.

Quite by coincidence, a true inferno had broken out within one of the most iconic symbols of modern Russia—Ostankino Tower, at seventeen hundred feet, the tallest building in all of Europe. When it was built, it was the tallest structure in the world. An architectural wonder, the tower—essentially a radio tower that also housed a restaurant and an observation deck—had been built in the late sixties, but was under constant reconstruction and repair—perhaps making it an even more apt emblem of the Russian state.

And now, suddenly, it was burning. Huge plumes of flame burst out from the structure into an otherwise pristine sky, billowing black smoke filled the air for miles in every direction. According to the news, the conflagration had begun around fifteen hundred feet off the ground, somewhere between the fancy, upscale restaurant and the popular circular observation platform. The fire's start had been followed by a small explosion that had caused the elevator that ran up the spine of the great tower to suddenly snap free. It plummeted to the ground, crashing and instantly killing an operator. At least three other people had already died, and it looked as though it was going to be some time before the emergency crews would be able to get control of the flames, because of the high winds at that height. And also because the only way up involved a winding, narrow staircase, since the elevator was now a shattered, mangled steel coffin embedded in the ground.

Badri had been glued to the coverage most of the afternoon, a part of him marveling at yet another tragedy having struck the Russian nation. Then the phone call had come in, and one of Berezovsky's numerous assistants rushed the receiver to where he was sitting. Hearing that voice on the other end of the line had immediately sent a jolt into Badri's stomach. He considered himself a tough character—and certainly, anyone who had spent time with him would have backed that description wholeheartedly—and yet, when the head of the FSB called, even a man like Badri couldn't help but think the worst.

Badri did his best to swallow his fear as he asked the FSB Director Nikolai Patrushev if the call had something to do with the burning tower—which ORT owned—but the official was noncommittal, allowing the Georgian to believe whatever made him feel better. After a pause, Patrushev then suggested that Badri head right over to the FSB offices for a conversation. Badri was in no mood to chat, but it was exactly the sort of "suggestion" he had made in various business situations over the years—the sort of suggestion a prudent man didn't ignore.

On the way over to Lubyanka Square and the forbidding building that housed the FSB offices, Badri played over the meeting his partner Berezovsky had endured the week before. Unfortunately, Berezovsky's emotions had still been riding high, and much of what he had communicated to Badri had been incomprehensible and contradictory. But the gist of it was clear enough: Berezovksy believed that he was going to be handled like Gusinsky. It wasn't clear if Putin had actually uttered words to that effect, but Berezovsky believed that the state wanted their shares in ORT and that Berezovsky had gone much too far with his coverage of the *Kursk* incident.

When Badri arrived at the FSB headquarters, he was led directly to the head office on the third floor, the same corner real estate that had been home to so many infamous leaders of the FSB and KGB before it, including Vladimir Putin himself. And, to the Georgian's surprise, when he got to the office, it wasn't just Patrushev who he saw was waiting for him, in a corner by the window behind the desk, but also the president himself, right up front, just a few feet inside the door.

Badri's heart beat heavily in his chest, but he did his best to remain calm. The president began the conversation, while the FSB director simply sat by the window, watching quietly. Putin started off by demanding to know what strange game Berezovsky was play-ing; the president insisted that Badri needed to talk sense into his emotional partner, that they were deadly serious about Berezovsky stepping away from ORT. At some point in the conversation, Badri believed Putin used the term *clear out*, and when Badri asked the president to clarify what that might mean, Putin explained that no one man should have that sort of power over a television station, that the media had to be treated differently than other businesses.

From there, the conversation moved into a more intricate and specific conversation about what it would mean to completely clear out of ORT—by selling their forty-nine percent. Who might pur-chase it from them? Which companies might be willing to pay a fair price? Apparently, the government had given this much thought, and it seemed like there would be no other way for them to continue, as long as Berezovksy's arrogance and stubbornness did not allow him to take a step back. He couldn't be trusted to stay away from sticking his nose in the day-to-day operations of the station, which meant he wasn't going to be allowed to keep his stake for much longer.

From the moment Putin began speaking, Badri knew that this was not an argument or even a true conversation. This decision had already been made. The wind was blowing in an obvious direction. Badri was pragmatic enough not to disagree, and he was ready to accept a situation he could not change. By the meeting's end, he had resigned himself to dealing with the practicalities; ORT would have to be sold, it was just a matter of how much they could get.

When Putin was finished speaking, he moved to shake Badri's hand. As they said their good-byes, Badri shyly apologized for his casual outfit. He explained that he had thought that perhaps he was going to be arrested, so he had dressed for the occasion.

Putin squeezed the Georgian's shoulder as he led him to the door.

"We are friends, Badri, go into any other business and I'll continue to support you. But if you stay in television, you will be my enemy."

Badri had communicated many messages in his career. He had delivered them to managers of oil refineries, to dangerous men from the aluminum industry, to dirty car salesmen, even to terrorist warlords.

There was no doubt in his mind; he and his partner had just been given such a message.

CHAPTER TWENTY-FOUR

October 30, 2000,

Private Terminal, Sheremetiezo Airport, Moscow

FOR ONE OF THE first times in Berezovsky's life, the Oligarch was moving slowly. Each step was like pulling his shoes out of thick mud, while his bare right hand clung numbly to the cold metal railing at his side. The retractable stairway leading up to his private Bombardier Global Express jet was barely taller than he was, but those six narrow steps felt like the longest journey Berezovsky had ever taken.

The icy breeze pulled at the high collar of his overcoat, each breath stinging his lungs with a palpable mingling of scents: jet fuel, car exhaust, cigarette smoke. And yet, above all, it smelled like Moscow, the city that had been his home for so long. The place where he had built an empire, bought a government—and now he was leaving.

He had fought this moment as long as he could. Putin's warning—or threat, as Berezovsky saw it—reiterated to Badri at the FSB offices might have scared off a more prudent man. But Berezovsky had at first seen it as another challenge, another obstacle in his path. On September 4, after those fateful meetings, Berezovsky had gone on the offensive, although Badri pleaded with him to tread carefully.

He had published an open letter in his newspaper, *Kommersant*, detailing Putin's attack, as he saw it—outlining how the president and the government had demanded that the businessman give up his legally owned shares in ORT or face destruction. In the letter he had demanded that the government should instead give up its own holding in the television station, that Russia needed a truly free press, and that Putin's efforts against him were part of an overall effort to take control of all the media in the country.

Berezovsky had known that publishing such an open letter, a direct attack on the president, was incredibly risky. But he had hoped that the act would bring the people of Russia to his side, as well as the journalistic community. And yet the blow had turned out to be another miscalculation. No matter how he tried to couch the battle he was engaged in, he was an Oligarch facing off against a popular president.

The next move had been Putin's, and it had again taken Berezovsky entirely by surprise. On October 17, the Oligarch was paid a visit by the prosecutor general, who arrived at the Logovaz Club accompanied by a squad of federal agents. Although he wasn't there to arrest Berezovsky, he had come to ask questions about Aeroflot—something that Berezovsky had thought he had dealt with before Putin's ascension to the presidency. The prosecutor general had suggested that Berezovsky would likely face criminal charges again, that his involvement in the national airline involved financial fraud and currency smuggling. Furthermore, they said that businessman Nikolai Glushkov, one of Berezovsky's close friends, whom Berezovsky had placed in charge of Aeroflot management, was also in danger of a criminal investigation.

Another barely veiled threat—and this time not only against the Oligarch himself, but against a friend and colleague. Berezovsky had been unable to protect Litvinenko, a relative nobody, from eight months in prison—and at the time, Putin had been only the head of the FSB. He had no doubt that if the president wanted to put Glushkov in irons, there was little he could do to stop him.

The government wasn't finished with him yet. The very next day, Berezovsky received notice that he was being evicted from his beloved dacha in Alexandrovka, which, though technically state-owned, Berezovksy had been legally renting since 1994. The notice came with no explanation or leave for petition; Berezovsky simply needed to vacate the premises, immediately.

Even so, even through the Aeroflot threat and the eviction, Berezovsky had intended to continue the fight. But on October 26, Putin had made his intentions clear in a way that Berezovsky couldn't ignore. On his way to an official visit to France, the president had given an interview to the newspaper *Le Figaro*, speaking in words as clear and harsh as a Moscow snow:

"Generally, I don't think that the state and the businessmen are natural enemies. Rather, the state has a cudgel in its hands that you use to hit just once, but on the head. We haven't used this cudgel yet. We've just brandished it, which is enough to keep someone's attention. The day we get really angry, we will not hesitate to use it. It is inadmissible to blackmail the state. If necessary, we will destroy those instruments that allow this blackmail."

According to *The Moscow Times*, which published the exchange in its entirety the next day, there was no doubt whom Putin had been speaking to; the *Times* identified Berezovsky by name, and referred to the statement as both a warning and a threat.

After that interview, Berezovsky had no doubt—he wasn't just in danger of losing his dacha, his stakes in ORT and Aeroflot—he was facing actual, physical danger. Even Roman Abramovich, a usually calm and rational voice, who had been disturbed by Berezovsky's handling of the *Kursk* incident and had tried to play the role of peacemaker with the Kremlin on numerous occasions, had admitted that Putin's interview seemed threatening. For his part, the young entrepreneur still believed that Berezovksy and the government could find a way to work things out, if only Berezovksy could take a step back and calm his emotions. After all, Berezovsky and the president had once been friends; Abramovich believed that it was Putin who felt betrayed, that Berezovsky had turned on the harddriving president, rather than the other way around.

But Berezovksy was certain that they were now well past the point of apologies and stepping back. He could not rid his thoughts of that cudgel, in Putin's hand, raised over his head. He had survived assassination attempts before, but this was the president of Russia, speaking in his own, direct words.

On that breezy airfield outside of Moscow, moving slowly up the metal stairs, Berezovsky paused to take one last breath. He was near the top step now. He could already feel the warmth coming from inside the lavishly appointed jet. He could smell the leather of the interior and the slight wisp of floral perfume from one of his statuesque flight attendants. And yet his shoulders sagged beneath his coat.

Despite everything, a part of him wanted to stay and fight, but even Badri agreed, the danger was too great. As he stood there, about to take that final step, his hands tightened even harder against the steel of the handrail. Putin had a cudgel and he was not afraid to use it; but Boris Berezovsky had been underestimated before.

Gusinsky had underestimated him and his men had ended up facedown in the snow. Korzhakov had underestimated him, and he had gone from Yeltsin's right hand to sudden unemployment. Even George Soros had underestimated him.

Berezovsky raised his chin, and a slight, defiant smile moved across his lips.

For a man with enough money in the bank, and the right sort of determination, the world could be a very small place—and an ocean, a very narrow distance.

PART THREE

It's a hard winter, when one wolf eats another.

—OLD RUSSIAN PROVERB

CHAPTER TWENTY-FIVE

November or December 2000,
Cap d'Antibes, Côte d'Azur, France

"**Q**UITE AN ARMY YOU'VE built, Boris," Badri murmured as he stood next to Berezovsky at the rear of the cavernous entrance hall to the oceanfront mansion, watching the nearby security team as they went about their protocols. "You would think we were about to be invaded by the Northern Fleet."

Berezovsky tried to smile, though he wasn't exactly in the mood for jokes. He felt a warm hand at his waist, and he tried to relax his posture, glancing back at Yelena, his girlfriend and cohabitant in exile. She was a striking sight, as usual, thin and beautiful, in her heels much taller than the Oligarch, with cascading, long brown hair and skin the color and texture of porcelain. A true natural beauty, and more and more his partner, although technically not his wife, she was the mother of two of his children. He had had two wives already, and in fact was still married to the second one, and he had sired two children with each of them, as well. Yet his feelings for Yelena were special. She was more than just an accoutrement, part of the trappings of paradise he had surrounded himself with since his exile from Moscow. She was significant in a way no material possession could be.

"You can't accuse a man of being paranoid after the second assassination attempt," Berezovsky responded, but Badri only shrugged.

"An army can't protect you from yourself, мой друг, my friend."

Boris felt Yelena's hand tighten a bit against his waist, and he patted her arm. She sighed, and then signaled toward one of the nearby house staff to start circulating cocktails. Lunch had ended just a few minutes earlier, and yet Berezovsky's stomach still felt tight and shriveled. He hadn't eaten much in the week since he had left Moscow.

The Oligarch had heard Badri's—and others'—words numerous times before. Many people believed he possessed a self-destructive streak. Even he agreed that he allowed his emotions to get out of control, which sometimes sabotaged his own efforts. Over the course of the past week, Badri had been like a broken record, reasserting again and again that Berezovsky had pushed things to this point. That he had allowed his anger and his arrogance to drive a wedge between himself and the government, one that could only have resulted in exile.

The tension in his body, the way his intestines seemed to coil in on themselves as he stood in the great hall—the entrance to a truly magnificent mansion, the sort of castle most people never set foot in, and only a few owned—told him that in many ways his Georgian friend was correct. It wasn't simply that he was his own worst enemy, but it was the way perception could become such a skewed and dangerous beast.

One man's exile, another man's paradise. His Château de la Garoupe was one of the most exquisite buildings in the South of France. Built on two idyllic hectares at the tip of the Antibes in the early nineteen hundreds, it had been specifically designed to show-case the spectacular setting—a marble-and-stone palace filled with rustic touches, many of the furnishings dating back to the Renais-sance. The grounds included some of the most beautiful gardens in the world, built at the top of magnificent stepped terraces that led down to the ocean.

The entrance hall itself, where the three of them stood, was a marvel of architecture, more stone and marble, fronted by three archways that led out to the receiving driveway. The dozen well-armed security guards—a mix of French and Israeli ex-army profes-sionals—did not detract from the elegance of the scenery.

The château was only one of three properties Berezovksy had bought back in 1997, at the beginning of his rise in fortune, for more than 120 million French francs. In the beginning, the château had been a place where Berezovsky could go to settle his thoughts, to take time out from the politics and the business, to simply revel in what he had built. He had come from nothing and was living like royalty in the most pristine setting on earth.

But here he was, barely three years later, twisted up like a spring. An exile, forced out of Moscow, and worse yet, out of his position, out of his power, by a man he believed he had partially created, his own personal Gollum. Badri would have called his thoughts foolish, more self-destructive mental masturbation. *Again, a matter of that beast, perception.*

But, Berezovsky might have countered, it was a healthy delu-sion that had been the engine that have driven him so far. Only a deluded man could believe it was possible to buy a government or build an empire out of Lada automobiles.

As Yelena handed him a drink off a silver tray carried by one of their staff, Berezovsky did his best to clear these thoughts from his mind. Paranoid or self-destructive and deluded, Berezovsky still believed he could trust the man they were expecting, Roman Abramovich. He was not an enemy.

A slight commotion from the security staff at the front of the great hall announced that the visitor had finally arrived. Berezovsky guessed that it hadn't been a simple trip from Moscow. To get to this wealthy playland, situated halfway between Nice and Cannes, meant traveling to private airfields and often at least one helicopter pad and then being chauffeured in limousines. Such were the difficulties of supreme fortune.

The front doors were opened from the outside, and Roman Abramovich stepped through into the hall. His sandy fluff of hair had been touched by the salty wind of the French Riviera, and he was casually dressed. Even so, he looked every bit the businessman and walked with the purposeful gait of someone moving from one important matter to another. Berezovsky recognized that walk—in fact, a part of him believed he had invented it.

Abramovich did not pause to marvel at the Renaissance furniture or the rare artwork on the walls. He had been to the château before. After all, it was the bags of cash that he had delivered to the Logovaz Club that had purchased the place, though Berezovsky thought of every inch of it his own. When Abramovich reached their group, he shook both Berezovsky's and Badri's hands, then kissed Yelena hello. Over the years, Abramovich's wife and Berezovsky's girlfriend had grown close. At times, the two couples had made quite the foursome, traveling to ski resorts and Caribbean retreats. That now seemed like a long time ago. Still, Yelena smiled warmly at the young man, then led them all out through the back of the château to the terrace.

Even in the fall and winter, the grand terrace doors were always open; Yelena liked to let the breeze from the ocean play across the marble floors and vaulted ceilings. The air was a little cold outside, even for this time of year, but Berezovsky hardly noticed. He was staying only a foot behind Abramovich, leading by way of a hand on the younger man's shoulder, navigating their progress toward a group of chairs in a far corner of the stone patio. Once outside, Yelena immediately wanted to leave them to their business, but Berezovsky signaled for her to settle herself at a long dining table instead, about five yards from where the men would be sitting. She would be too far away to hear the conversation, but close enough that Berezovsky could still see her. Looking at her was a way of centering himself, of keeping his emotions grounded. At the moment, he was afraid that he was on the verge of losing control once again.

No matter how much he trusted Roman Abramovich, no matter how much he thought of the entrepreneur as a partner, he believed Roman had come to France to discuss the sale of Berezovsky's share of ORT, the television network he had used to put Yeltsin and Putin in power. Badri had been going back and forth between them since the *Kursk* incident, and it was Badri who, after his own meeting with Putin at the FSB headquarters, had presented Abramovich with the proposition that had now brought them together.

As usual, the three men dispensed with pleasantries quickly and then got directly to the point. Berezovsky felt a dark storm rising inside him. Badri and Abramovich seemed to be talking around him, as if he were a petulant child who had brought them to this point— a place where none of them seemed to want to be. And yet here they were.

According to Abramovich, he had initially resisted the idea of stepping in as buyer of the TV network; he had no interest in being in the media business and no use for Berezovsky's shares. Between

Sibneft and the aluminum industry, his hands were full, his attentions stretched to its limit. But in Moscow, and at the Kremlin, he was, in his words, always in the shadow of Boris Berezovsky; as long as Berezovsky held onto his percentage of ORT and was an enemy of the Kremlin, it was bad for Sibneft's business and dangerous for Abramovich's future prospects.

Badri seemed to agree. The situation was dire, and he was extremely pessimistic about the way things were heading. For that reason, Badri had set out to convince Abramovich to take the ORT shares off their hands, to take the pressure of the negative relationship with the exiled Oligarch away from Sibneft, and to lower the heat on Berezovsky himself. Both Badri and Abramovich hoped and believed that Berezovsky would eventually calm down. Perhaps one day things could return to normal, and he could even get his ORT shares back.

Reluctant though he was, Abramovich had even taken the step to meet with Putin, to see if such a deal would be acceptable to the Kremlin. The president had informed him that he really didn't care who took over Berezovsky's forty-nine percent of the television network. The only thing that mattered to Putin was that Berezovksy had been using the media empire for his own purposes, and this needed to stop. Putin had apparently gone even further—he had asked why a rising star like Abramovich was sticking his neck out to help Berezovsky—and Roman had only explained that he was trying to do his mentor a favor, that Berezovsky had been a helpful ally in building Sibneft, that he wasn't an enemy, despite his recent behavior. Putin had shrugged this off, but Abramovich had left the meeting with the feeling that his purchase of ORT might smooth the situation to some degree.

Berezovsky wasn't sure what he thought about the idea of his protégé meeting with the president to discuss taking away his company, but as the talk on the terrace of his château now turned to numbers—one hundred fifty million dollars, the sum that Badri and Abramovich had negotiated—Berezovsky's anger began to rise. It was a lot of money, but to Berezovsky, it was still a forced sale. In his eyes, Putin had threatened him until he had fled in fear of his safety, and now Abramovich was going to take his company. He definitely didn't care for Abramovich and Badri's explanations—that the price, one hundred fifty million, was more than he would get from the state or from any other buyer, and that they were actually doing him a favor with such a deal, that it would be enough money to continue funding his extravagant lifestyle, the elegance around them.

Looking at the French garden spread out below them, the thirty-foot-tall rosebushes, the terraced landscape leading down to the azure water, he guessed that all Abramovich and Badri saw were numbers on a ledger. But Berezovsky didn't see numbers, or even the beauty of the place—he saw Aeroflot criminal charges, Putin hitting him over the head with a damn cudgel. He saw the threats, the blackmail, the exile, and forced sale. Even though Abramovich might not have been using such words, might not have mentioned Nikolai Glushkov, prison, or potential arrest, Berezovsky believed his protégé was becoming aligned with the Kremlin.

Berezovsky wasn't selling ORT because he wanted to, but because he had no other choice. He believed that Putin would use Aeroflot to go after him with criminal charges, and that Glushkov would rot in jail if he didn't acquiesce even though he had declared his innocence.

And even though Abramovich's tone might not have been threatening, his demeanor certainly seemed to have changed. In the past, Berezovsky had always seen the young man as humble, deferential, even obsequious. Berezovsky had been the mentor, the powerful kingmaker, and Abramovich had been the young, ambitious charge. The way Berezovsky saw it, he had taken Abramovich under his wing, and had helped him build himself into a successful businessman.

But now, sitting outside the château, it appeared that their roles had reversed. Abramovich believed he was buying ORT to protect and help Berezovsky. Abramovich was friendly with the Kremlin, ran a huge oil company, and was going to take ORT out of Berezovsky's hands.

Abramovich may have believed he was acting in all of their best interests, but as Berezovsky saw it, Abramovich had decided that Berezovsky was a threat to his business, a heavy weight hanging around his neck, and he was going to free himself by taking Berezovsky out of the equation, shoveling him off into his quiet exile. Putin was the future, and for Abramovich to continue to thrive in Russia, he needed to be at peace with the Kremlin. Which meant drawing a line between him and his former mentor.

In his head, Berezovsky was reassessing his relationship with the younger man, rethinking all of his previous opinions. He had considered the two of them close friends, in the way of a mentor and a student. But perhaps he hadn't fully taken into account the differences between himself and the younger man—not just in their personalities, but in their histories—*generational* differences. Berezovsky believed himself to be a true capitalist, a believer in what he called democracy, in modernity—but he couldn't deny that a part of him was a product of the older, Soviet era. And he was also, at heart, an academic. Abramovich shared his outsider status, but the younger man had been formed in the chaos of their nation's new capitalism, his business sense honed in the streets and alleys of post-perestroika Russia.

Berezovsky had put his trust in Abramovich, and he wondered now, had this been yet another miscalculation? One day, would he see this moment as the end of their friendship, and the beginning of a vaster betrayal?

Abramovich believed that the rift between them had begun after the *Kursk* tragedy. Abramovich had told Badri many times that he thought Berezovsky was misusing the event to take his shots at Putin, that he was being hostile at exactly the wrong time, that he was using a national drama for a personal attack. But Berezovsky felt that this was beside the point, and it wasn't Abramovich's place to criticize but to support. And if the rift had begun then, with the *Kursk*, well, here in this beautiful setting, in a place so evocative of a heaven built on his success, this moment seemed to be the final shattering of what was left of the ties between them. What Abramovich wasn't saying—but what Berezovsky knew, deep in his soul—was that the older Oligarch wasn't useful to the younger man anymore. A krysha in exile wasn't a krysha anymore—he was a liability. Abramovich's 150-million-dollar offer was a quick and simple attempt to get rid of this liability.

Well, Berezovsky didn't intend to go quietly, to slink off into exile because he no longer seemed *useful*. And Abramovich was dead wrong if he believed that a check—even such a large one— would solve their situation. Threats, money, explanations, whether they came from Roman Abramovich, or Vladimir Putin himself, wouldn't change a damn thing.

Boris Berezovsky wasn't going anywhere.

CHAPTER TWENTY-SIX

Winter 2001,

Serpentine Bridge, Kensington Gardens, London

*T*HERE'S NO SUCH THING *as an ex-KGB agent. . . .*

Alexander Litvinenko had to smile at the ironic words reverberating through his thoughts, as he leaned against the railing of the aging stone bridge, looking down into the dark swirls of the Serpentine Lake. The artificial body of water had been dug sometime in the early eighteenth century by Queen Caroline. It squatted directly between the Italian Gardens—often brimming with tourists, though quite empty this deep into winter—and the swimming area known as Lansbury's Lido. The lake itself fed underground into the Thames, which ran like a twisting snake through the bustling, cosmopolitan city of London, the metropolis that Litvinenko now called home. As of late, he'd often found himself here, on this bridge; but this was the first time that precise thought about the eternity of belonging to the KGB had entered his head. Funny, that a quote attributed to Vladimir Putin, supposedly uttered sometime during his campaign for president, would seem so apt to Litvinenko, living in exile, at Putin's hand.

Litvinenko tapped his fingers on the attaché case that sat atop the ledge of the railing, right next to him. The case was full of files, many of them loose documents Litvinenko had collected for a book he was working on, together with another of Boris Berezovsky's many protégés. Also in the attaché were other files of a more private nature, information for a project he was working on that involved the Italian government, and assistance he would soon be providing them, in identifying former FSB agents in Rome.

Litvinenko had to give Putin credit, the man wasn't wrong. Here Litvinenko was no longer an agent and yet was still practicing his stagecraft, with fingers in so many different pies. A lifetime away from Moscow, and he was still surrounded by the same sort of people with whom he had always surrounded himself—men with secrets to trade or sell, often dangerous individuals who lived in the gray edges of the real world, operating in the dark corners, mostly invisible to the average citizens moving past.

On cue, a taxi rumbled behind him, traversing the center lane of the bridge that divided sprawling Hyde Park from Kensington Gardens. The bulbous, insect-like vehicle was no doubt filled with tourists or perhaps carried a financial worker to the office. Whoever it was in that taxi would have no idea that the man they'd just passed on the bridge was a former spy who had just completed a terrifying sprint to freedom, from halfway across the world.

Litvinenko had no doubt that, had he remained in Moscow—perhaps even a day longer—he would have been thrown back in prison, or worse. His official asylum in London might not protect him forever, but it was a fresh start—and he owed everything, as usual, to his patron, Boris Berezovsky.

A short family vacation to Sochi on the Black Sea had been Litvinenko's cover for his escape. Using an identification card from his days as an undercover agent in Chechnya, he had managed to land travel documents; then he made a terrifying journey to Turkey, followed by a flight to Heathrow. Once Litvinenko arrived in London, Berezovsky, who had also moved there, had taken over arrangements. Without any prodding, the Oligarch had set up Litvinenko and his family in an apartment in Kensington, renting him a flat that might not have been luxurious, but compared nicely to his old apartment in Moscow. Kensington itself was a sparkling, upper-class corner of London, bordered by the same gardens that now splayed out behind him, and right up next to the center of the bustling city.

Berezovsky's largesse hadn't ended there; the Oligarch was also providing Litvinenko with a salary of five thousand pounds a month. His job description hadn't ever been spelled out, but the way he saw it, he was essentially an "associate on call"; if Berezovsky ever needed his particular skill set, he would be available, no questions asked. He hadn't taken over Berezovsky's security concerns—the Oligarch used more seasoned professionals available for that—but Berezovsky liked having him around. Perhaps he believed that an ex-FSB man would be helpful in identifying threats that a bodyguard might miss. To paraphrase Putin, once an agent, always an agent, and Litvinenko had a particular ability to sniff out other members of his tribe.

The fact that both he and Berezovsky were residing in the UK was one of those strange coincidences of timing that seemed to speak to a greater destiny. Litvinenko had no doubt this destiny involved both of them, albeit at different heights. Berezovsky's flight from Russia, via France, had nothing to do with the FSB agent's troubles with Putin, but they had certainly faced off against the same enemy.

Both of them were now starting fresh, because of the actions of the Kremlin. Shortly after arriving in the UK, the Oligarch had sold off his entire stake in the television network ORT to his young partner, Roman Abramovich. The sale had not gone down easy; Berezovsky had resisted, even refused—until halfway into December, when Putin had stepped up his pressure. Nikolai Glushkov, Berezovsky's friend and business colleague at Aeroflot, was arrested. Berezovsky had immediately seen the action as the conclusion of an implied threat, although it certainly might have been a coincidence. Either way, Berezovsky had the notion that by selling his shares in ORT, he could help Glushkov gain his freedom from prison—and shield himself from criminal charges.

Berezovsky's notion had been wrong. Even after Berezovsky had begun divesting himself of ORT, Glushkov remained in prison, which had enraged Berezovsky, and had also hardened his resolve to continue to fight against Putin and the Kremlin. But that fight would have to take place from exile, gilded by the influx of money that Abramovich had helpfully provided.

Berezovsky knew how to live in style, that was for sure. The Oligarch had set himself up in a twenty-million-pound mansion in Surrey and surrounded himself with a phalanx of bodyguards that followed him everywhere. He was renting an office in Mayfair, and traveled in a six-hundred-thousand-dollar, bulletproof Maybach. They both knew that being in London didn't make either of them safe. There was nowhere that was entirely out of reach of the FSB. But with the right security, and a careful eye for detail, Litvinenko felt sure that the two of them—Oligarch and "ex"-agent—could find a way to thrive.

To this end, Litvinenko planned to continue living the way he always had—in the gray edges, where his particular skills made him valuable. Since arriving in London, he had searched out as many like-minded actors as he could—ex-agents, Russian ex-pat "businessmen," black marketeers, and even political refugees—including one high-profile Chechen leader who had once been labeled a terrorist by Litvinenko's former employers. These were Litvinenko's colleagues, his dark coterie of friends. With them, he felt at home, and through them, he was finding his way in his new environment, socially and financially.

At that particular moment, he was on the Serpentine Bridge waiting for one of those ex-agents—one of the handful of contacts he had developed, whom he never called by name—who would soon be arriving to trade information. Information, in the gray world where Litvinenko plied his trade, was the truest form of currency. It could be exchanged for real wealth, and when applied correctly, it could mean the difference between life and death. Litvinenko saw himself as an expert at procuring information—and he had no doubt, sooner or later, the right information could make all the difference, both for himself, and for his generous patron.

Looking up from the dark water, out across the sparkling lights of Kensington, the brightly burning facades of the various expensive hotels and high-end shops, Litvinenko's smile widened. Some aspects of the Western world fit his personality even better than the East. Certainly, Berezovsky too had to feel at home, in a place that seemed to live and breathe capitalism, pulsing in its incessant quest for money. But in the end, it was beyond Litvinenko's pay grade to try to understand what really made the Oligarch tick.

Marina still liked to joke that Litvinenko and Berezovsky were from different worlds—that the ex-agent was a member of the chorus, while Berezovsky was one of the leads—but in London, in the West, that division seemed to mean so much less. Litvinenko and Berezovsky both had opportunities ahead of them—as long as they learned how to correctly apply their particular skills.

Another car passed behind Litvinenko, throwing up dust and

gravel—and then he heard footsteps on the bridge to his left. He gazed through the growing darkness as the shape of a man in an overcoat pulled tight at the neck and waist emerged. The man carried an attaché case of his own somewhere inside that coat, and Litvinenko felt that old tingle rising inside his veins. It didn't matter where he stood on a map, this, in itself, was *home*.

He laughed, wondering what the handful of tourists in the distance, wandering through Kensington Gardens, might think of the two men on the bridge trading cases.

Most likely, they would think nothing at all.

CHAPTER TWENTY-SEVEN

January 10, 2001,

Megève, Rhône-Alpes Region, France

BORIS CROUCHED LOW IN the backseat of the armored limousine, his face inches from the bulletproof side window, to stare up at the gunmetal canopy of clouds. He couldn't be sure how long the car had been parked in that spot; he had spent the first few minutes simply gazing at the crown of mountains that surrounded them, his thoughts lost in the swirl of snow that seemed to be blowing through the heliport from every conceivable angle.

Megève was beautiful and foreboding. Berezovsky had never seen anywhere quite like it. The tiny resort town perched at the very top of the French Alps, a frozen, high-altitude junction between a half-dozen ski resorts known only to the wealthiest. A desolate, yet somehow charming quaint little town that felt like it was situated at the apex of the world, with air so thin, it made him dizzy just rising to his feet.

It had taken a drive up the side of a mountain, along a narrow, sometimes single-lane road, looking out over sheer drops and hairpin turns stacked on top of each other, just to get there. Their progress had been so slow at times, and Berezovsky had been certain he would be the last to arrive at the summit. But somehow, he was now alone at the top, his only company the swirling snow. Only the soft purr of the limousine's engines broke the monotonous silence. Twice, his driver had gestured toward the small, enclosed café attached to the main building of the heliport, wordlessly asking if Berezovsky would be more comfortable waiting inside. And twice, Berezovsky had ignored him, his gaze pinned to the sky.

Even so, he heard their approach well before there was any change in the thick canopy of clouds. It began as a low throb, barely audible over the car's engine. Second by second, the throb grew into a low thunder, the unmistakable sound of oversize steel rotors fighting their way through moist mountain air.

It was another minute before the first helicopter burst through the clouds, curving down toward the nearest snow-covered helipad, bright red landing lights flashing like hungry irises, intent on nearby prey. The second helicopter swooped down out of the gray just a few minutes behind the first, touching down while the initial chopper's rotors were still spinning. A few more minutes, and finally the two sets of rotors had slowed enough for the helicopters to release their cargo. Almost in tandem, the passenger doors swung upward. Badri hopped out first, from the closest of the two, his head topped by a high, mink Cossack-style hat, most of his ruddy face obscured by the collar of a matching fur coat. Behind him, out of the second helicopter, came Roman Abramovich's party.

Berezovksy had expected that the young businessman would come alone, but the first person out of his passenger cabin was Abramovich's twentysomething Austrian chef. After the chef came Abramovich and his wife, Irina, each holding a hand of one of Abramovich's young children. *A true family affair.* In retrospect,

Berezovsky shouldn't have been surprised. Abramovich was on holiday, and he had flown in from the Château Sevan in Courcheval, where he often spent his winters. They had, in fact, chosen Megève because it was central to the vacation spots of the Alps. Although it now felt a little off: Berezovsky here in exile, Abramovich here in the midst of his family vacation.

Berezovksy watched from the car as Badri greeted Abramovich and his family. Then the small group headed together toward the warmth of the café. Only when they had reached the door, Badri holding it open for the handsome family, did Boris finally signal to his driver that it was time to escort him along.

♦ ♦ ♦

The café was small and quaint, walls mostly windows, tall glass panes looking out over the cascading mountains. The interior was filled with small metal tables surrounding a counter where you could order croissants, coffee, beer, and little else. But it was more than enough for their purposes. As Berezovsky entered, he saw that the chef, the wife, and the children had taken a table close to the window facing the two parked helicopters. Abramovich and the Georgian were on the other side of the café, far enough away that they wouldn't be overheard.

Berezovksy took his time reaching the table, and the conversation was already in full swing before he even sat down. Both sides had made it quite clear in advance that the meeting would be brief. Abramovich didn't want to take much time out of his family vacation, and Badri and Berezovsky weren't in Megève for a drawn-out negotiation. All the negotiations had already taken place; once again, Badri had been the go-between, traveling all over the world to meet with Abramovich and his bean counters. In Munich, Paris, London, they had worked over the numbers, back and forth, until there was nothing left to do but finalize the proposition. Perhaps this could have been done over the phone or on paper, but this uniquely Russian situation meant it should be done in the uniquely Russian style: face-to-face, not in a courtroom with lawyers, not with papers and signatures, but between men. Unlike what had transpired at the château in Antibes, this was truly a negotiation to end a relationship.

A uniquely Russian relationship.

"One billion, three hundred million," Abramovich said, as Berezovsky took his seat, and it almost seemed that the young man was tripping on the words.

It was a massive amount of money. At that moment, it could have been compared to the entire pension fund of the Russian Federation—maybe a quarter to half of the capitalization of Gazprom, the biggest gas company in Russia, and perhaps more than the entire current valuation of Sibneft itself. A king's ransom, an amount that would make Berezovsky one of the richest people in the world.

Berezovsky could tell by the way Badri's hands shook, clasped together in his lap, and the way a smile played at the corner of his lips, that his friend was equally affected by the amount. Badri had helped come up with the number, in consultation with Abramovich and Abramovich's right-hand man, Eugene. From what Badri had told Berezovsky, the number had been conceived by adding together the payments Abramovich had been making to Berezovsky each year, projecting a decade into the future, and then taking that calculation and massaging it into something that seemed fair.

The fact that Roman was willing to hand over this enormous lump sum, a historic amount by any consideration, was, in Badri's view, a testament to the younger man's respect and honor of their relationship, of what they had accomplished. Because, in Abramovich's mind, this was not a payment for future work, this was not a payment to purchase anything that Berezovsky now owned, it was a payment intended to dissolve their relationship.

What that meant, in a legal sense, was a matter of opinion. There were no official documents, there was no true paper trail that solidly defined what Berezovsky was owed or what part of Abramovich's empire he legitimately owned, but Abramovich had come up with a number he felt was fair, a payment he believed Berezovsky should accept, in return for the ending of their partnership, for lack of a better English word. One billion, three hundred million, to never owe anything again, to end all the payments, to end their business association.

Did Abramovich also see it as an end to their friendship, too, if that word meant anything in their relationship?

Berezovsky guessed that Abramovich would not have seen their friendship, now or before, in the same terms that Berezovsky had. To Abramovich, it had been a friendship built on payments, built on krysha. Berezovsky had been Abramovich's protection and his liaison to the Kremlin. He had helped Abramovich build an oil company. Was there a way to put a price on that? This wasn't an English or Western partnership, there weren't contracts or lawyers or signatures. Abramovich, in real, provable terms, wasn't buying shares—he was buying his freedom. And he was willing to pay more than a billion dollars for it.

The conversation shifted from the amount to the mechanism. A billion dollars was not an easy amount of cash to transfer; this was not going to be a matter of overstuffed suitcases delivered by little blond accountants.

Abramovich intended to make the payments from his aluminum profits, which brought in a steady cash flow. The payments would be made in bearer shares, exchanged through a Latvian bank.

As Badri and Abramovich worked out the details, Berezovsky was unusually silent. In the past, other than at the meeting at the château, when the three of them were together, Berezovsky would dominate the conversation. Never a man to stay in the background, he had always been described as a person who loved the sound of his own voice. But in this moment, he was swept up by complex feelings.

One billion, three hundred million. He should have been ecstatic, he should have been contemplating the future with a bankroll that seemed nearly bottomless. He could live like royalty for the rest of his life, his family would be wealthy for generations. He had gone from being an outsider, born a Jew in an anti-Semitic culture, relegated to special institutions on the outskirts of Russian life—to this moment, on the verge of becoming one of the wealthiest men alive. And yet, he couldn't feel happy.

Just as Abramovich had bought Berezovsky's share of ORT, Abramovich was now giving him this huge sum of money to make him go away. He wasn't offering him a billion dollars because he was significant or important—quite the opposite. *He was giving him this money because he was no longer relevant.*

For Berezovsky, it was the ultimate dishonor. He had always needed to be in the center of things, a lead actor, a major player.

If he wasn't important, he wasn't alive.

In the past, his enemies had tried to kill him with bombs, with FSB assassination orders, with criminal charges. He believed that now, they were trying to kill him with a big fat check.

And Berezovsky truly didn't know what he was going to do next. It was a strange feeling, being without a strategy, without a mission. It felt . . . wrong.

As the meeting drew to a close after less than an hour—one billion, three hundred million dollars offered and accepted—Roman Abramovich rose, signaling his family to put their coats back on for the short walk to the helicopter. Before he followed them outside, he paused to give both Badri and Berezovsky a final, warm, Russian embrace.

In the younger man's mind, perhaps, they were ending a business relationship, a krysha relationship, but they were parting at the same level of friendship they had always shared.

Abramovich would head back to Russia, his vacation over, and continue building his empire.

But where would Boris Berezovsky go next? Where did a man in exile go, after he was just handed a billion dollars?

CHAPTER TWENTY-EIGHT

October 25, 2003,
Novosibirsk, Siberia

BARELY TWO MINUTES AFTER five in the morning, the private Tupolev Tu-154 jet was coming down fast, its engines running on near fumes, as the pair of pilots in the cockpit searched for the strip of runway, through the thick, strangely orange fog of a predawn Siberian morning.

The flight from Moscow had been uneventful, and both pilots were extremely experienced, after multiple years in the private sector, and before that, stints in the Russian Air Force. But the refueling stop in such a heavy fog at this airport at the far edge of nowhere, a well-maintained set of runways laid down over a heavy, slick permafrost, bisecting the short distance between a fuel depot and a maintenance office, would have even the most experienced pilots' hearts pumping.

Nearby Novosibirsk was a burgeoning city, the third-most-populated metropolis in the country, after Moscow and St. Petersburg. But the Oligarch owner of the private jet—the pilots' boss—had chosen this particular airfield specifically because it was out of the way, and thus a little more protected. To the pilots, the team of heavily armed bodyguards taking up most of the jet's passenger cabin should have been protection enough, but this refueling stop was what the boss wanted, and thus it was what the boss was going to get.

After all, Khodorkovsky wasn't the richest man in Russia by accident. He had built his empire from nothing, in banking, oil—God only knew what else—and in the process had become one of the most well-known names in the country. That he was now on the government's shit list, for challenging the new regime at every step, meant little to the two men at the airplane's controls.

Like most people the pilots knew in these uncertain times, their political loyalties lay with whomever best filled their bank accounts. At the moment, they were happily pro-Oligarch, even if it meant the slight risk of ending up in a fiery ball in the middle of goddamn Siberia.

Thankfully, both pilots spotted the stretch of runway through the heavy fog at about the same moment. The lead pilot made the necessary adjustments to their descent, and they continued through their landing ritual. A few moments later, the tires touched concrete, coughing up a thin spray of ice and burning rubber. The engines slowed, the brakes kicking in, and the plane smoothly decelerated, as the pilots steered the plane toward the refueling station. Five more minutes, and they came to a complete stop. Outside on the tarmac, a gaggle of maintenance workers instantly moved into action.

"That's quite a crowd out there this morning," the copilot noticed, gesturing toward the view outside the cockpit.

The lead pilot squinted through the glass, realizing that his copilot was right. It seemed like almost three times as many refueling specialists as usual.

"Maybe it's the night and day shift, working together. A little bit of good luck, eh? Should have us out of here in no time. The boss will be happy about that."

"I'm not sure he has a happy setting—" the copilot started to say, but he never got the chance to finish.

There was a loud, sudden crash from behind the cockpit door at their backs, followed by intense shouting. Most of the words were muffled because of the thick reinforced door, but the lead pilot was certain he heard at least three words he understood: *Drop your weapons!*

And just as suddenly, a barrage of spotlights exploded across the tarmac in front of them, blasting everything in harsh, artificial light. The pilot covered his eyes with one hand, as the copilot hastily undid his seat belt.

There were more crashes from behind and then a pounding on the cockpit door. Someone was yelling for them to open it—immediately.

The lead pilot didn't see what choice they had. His hands were shaking as he reached for the door, and it took him an extra moment to finally get it open.

The two men standing in the doorway were large, wearing black masks, but all the pilot could see were the pair of submachine guns aimed at his chest. He quickly put his hands over his head. Then one of the men had him by the hair, and he was dragged out of the cockpit. Out of the corners of his eyes, he could see at least a dozen of similarly clad aggressors, crowding into the jet's passenger cabin. All the bodyguards were on the floor or seated, held at gunpoint. And at the very rear of the plane, being led out of his seat by more masked agents—the richest man in Russia.

November 8, 2003
7 Down Street, Mayfair, London

"That's the war we're fighting," Berezovsky nearly shouted, slamming a hand down against his desk, in his elegantly decorated office in Mayfair. "Khodorkovsky thought his billions would keep him safe, and that his popularity made him untouchable. And you see what happened? They took him right off his plane, and directly to prison. Do not pass go, do not collect your billion dollars. Money laundering, tax evasion, they are the bullets, but we all know who is holding the gun."

Berezovsky pointed at his own face, covered by a unique, somewhat obscene rubber mask with Vladimir Putin's face on it. To his surprise, the American journalist sitting across from him didn't smile at the display; in fact, she looked uncomfortable, if not a little bit terrified. Her own fault—she had been the one to ask about the mask, and Berezovsky had only put it on as a favor.

The likeness wasn't perfect, but the countenance was clearly recognizable. That he had been able to find a Putin mask in a local novelty shop had been a minor coup; maybe it showed that his new, adopted homeland truly did have a growing obsession with all things Russian. Likewise, Berezovsky had been amazed at how many newspapers his picture had made it into when he had donned the mask on his way out of a local courthouse, after one of his many extradition hearings.

The list of crimes he had been accused of back in Moscow seemed to grow every day he was in exile. Even though the American journalist had listed them twice already during the interview, Berezovsky himself couldn't even keep them straight. His exile had protected him. Sadly, his friend Glushkov, from Aeroflot, couldn't say the same thing. Selling ORT, then being paid off to "disappear" at the Megève heliport had done nothing to get his friend released. In fact, in a surreal state of affairs, just a few months after the Megève payout, Glushkov had found himself in even hotter water. During an approved visit to a hospital for blood work, he had reportedly staged an escape attempt, involving associates in phony guard uniforms; the escape had failed, and Glushkov had been grabbed by FSB agents. After this, he had been thrown back into jail, along with one of Berezovksy's security employees from ORT, Andrei Lugovoy, who had supposedly been helping Glushkov with his escape.

Worse yet, Badri had been tarred by that same brush, accused of aiding in the escape attempt. The loyal strongman had avoided arrest, having already joined Berezovsky in exile. Of course, the Russian press and the Kremlin had immediately assumed that Berezovsky had masterminded this failed escape attempt, part of the continuing effort to draw him as an enemy of the state, a despicable traitor.

Fair enough, he sometimes thought. For the past three years, since his exile began, he had indeed been engaged in an all-out publicity war with Putin—speaking about his perceived rival to anyone who would listen.

"Khodorkovsky learned how the legal system works in Moscow, didn't he?" Berezovsky continued, from behind the mask. "Now he's in a prison cell. He was the richest man in the country. Started off just like me—half Jewish, which meant he was Jewish enough to know that the only avenues open to him were in business. From banking, to Yukos oil. He should've left Russia when he had the chance. Instead, he stayed and tried to stand up to them. Look where it got him."

The same place, Berezovksy knew, where he would end up if

Russia ever managed to win its extradition battles. Fortunately for the Oligarch, not only had Berezovksy prevailed in court again and again—rubber mask and all—but just a week ago, he had been granted official political asylum in the UK. Rumors abounded that he had been turning over information to the British Secret Service in return for their protection, and he certainly liked the implications. Given how often he had been appearing in the British press, he felt once again that he had become a very important man. In the West, things were different; politics seemed secondary to money. And, at the moment, he had plenty of money to spend.

How much exactly, he couldn't be sure. He had bought a beautiful estate in nearby Surrey for more than twenty million dollars; ironically, not far from where Abramovich had one of his homes as well—though Abramovich still considered Moscow his main base of operations.

Berezovksy also traveled in style—his Maybach, his veritable army of bodyguards, his private jet, his own chefs, valets, and butlers. His real estate in France, a villa in the Caribbean, and he was continuously considering huge purchases all over the world. He was building a private art collection, and he had at least one yacht, perhaps three, though he couldn't be certain how many were under his name.

Of course, his yacht was nothing compared to Abramovich's—one of which was over 377 feet long, with a pair of helicopter pads and a huge swimming pool that turned into a dance floor. Nor could his real estate compare to his former protégé's—Abramovich was building a one-hundred-million-dollar palace in St. Barths and combining a block of apartments in Belgravia that could one day be worth twice that. Berezovsky might have a private jet, but Abramovich had a 767. And Abramovich had recently made the ultimate purchase, the storied Chelsea Football Club, probably worth over a billion dollars on its own.

Berezovsky knew, the fact that he could list everything that Abramovich owned—or was going to own—was a symptom of his rising obsession with the man, which had been building since their meeting at that heliport in Megève. Badri had told him many times he should simply let it go—that they were all wealthy now, that he and Badri had been paid an enormous sum—split between them, though they kept much of their assets intermingled—to end their krysha obligations, at least as much as was fair.

Badri, a much less ostentatious man by nature, had been using his money much differently. While he had put some of it into investments such as the Buddha Bar in New York, he had made his primary home in Georgia, the ex-Russian province of his birth, rather than in England or the United States. Berezovsky had pushed his friend into politics in the breakaway territory—using some of his own money to help Badri fund the Rose Revolution, which had put one of Badri's friends and colleagues—and a democratic, liberalizing influence—Mikheil Saakashvili, a pro-West candidate who was only thirty-six, into the Georgian presidency.

Badri—and Berezovsky—were once again close to power, though in Georgia instead of Russia. Badri was considered the richest man in that province, beloved by his people. In that role, Badri had also set off to try to repair his relationship with the Kremlin, even reaching out to Putin himself—and he had suggested many times that Berezovsky give up his war of words and make amends.

But Berezovsky refused; he saw himself on a sort of holy mission. Putin was his nemesis, and he was going to use every minute and every dollar he had to try to bring down the president.

Berezovsky removed the Putin mask and placed it on his desk, as the American journalist scribbled notes into her legal pad. Berezovsky had long ago lost count of the number of interviews he had given; he had been willing to speak to just about anyone who would listen. One of the things he loved most about the West was the hunger of the press for a juicy story—and the multitude of organizations that would use just about any headline to sell a newspaper. If anything, Berezovsky had been born to dole out headlines. His verbal challenges to Putin had gone from recounting the supposed threats and brutal political machinations that had led to his own London exile to outlining his personal quest to fund a violent revolution against the Russian president.

And Berezovsky wasn't just mouthing words to the press in England, he had surrounded himself with like-minded agitators: Litvinenko, of course, as well as the young agent's friends in exile, and anyone else who had a beef with the Russian president. Berezovksy was their nexus, their continuous source of funding, and his office at 7 Down Street had become their central gathering place.

He knew that his words and actions were riling the Kremlin and his enemies back in Russia. Berezovsky believed there had been at least one more assassination attempt against him—evidence of which had led to his political asylum—and he expected more to come. But he didn't care. The very fact that they were going after him meant he was still significant.

He didn't expect to be able to topple Putin overnight; but the extradition hearings and Berezovsky's political asylum was proof that the Russian president didn't have the power to simply wave his hand and have Berezovsky sent to prison, as he had done with Khodorkovsky. It was a facet of one of the other characteristics that Berezovksy loved most about the West, and the UK in particular, the powerful, historic legal system.

He had learned that a man with money, and access to good lawyers, could go after just about any prize. In earlier days, he had filed suit against *Forbes* magazine for an article written by an American journalist named Paul Klebnikov, which Berezovsky felt linked him to a number of murders, and which claimed he had developed a Mafia-like presence in the Russian government. The article—and a book the journalist had written along the same topic—had referred to Berezovsky as the "Godfather of The Kremlin." Even though *Forbes*, at the time, had barely any readers in the UK, Berezovsky had been able to use England's lax libel laws to put immense pressure on the journalist and the magazine—taking advantage of what many legal experts called "libel tourism" to bring the suit into a court system that seemed most likely to rule in the Oligarch's favor. The dispute ran for years, finally ending in 2003 with a partial retraction from Forbes and an acknowledgement that Berezovsky's business partner Glushkov did not have a conviction for theft of state property.

Since then, Berezovsky had been a party in lawsuit after lawsuit, some having to do with business dealings and loan repayments, some trending more personal. Eventually, he expected also to be in a courtroom facing at least one of his ex-wives. But all in all, he considered the Western legal system another weapon in his armament.

He was still adjusting to life in exile, but he believed that by combining Russian strategies and persistence with modern, Western tools—he could stay more relevant than even Abramovich could ever have suspected.

Badri might have seen his passion—his holy mission—as another sign of his self-destructiveness, but Berezovksy believed it was quite the opposite. His obsessions—with Putin, with Abramovich, with his own importance—were keeping him alive.

CHAPTER TWENTY-NINE

November 1, 2006,

Itsu Sushi, 167 Piccadilly, London

IT WAS A LITTLE after ten minutes past three in the afternoon, and Alexander Litvinenko suddenly found himself surrounded by a little too much plastic, a little too many bright neon swatches of color for his tastes. But he had to admit, the sushi wasn't half bad, and the bustle of people passing by on Piccadilly, outside the front windows of the restaurant, provided a pleasant contrast to his lunch companion.

He'd gotten to know the man he called Mario fairly well over the past couple of years. As usual, the Italian looked like he had just stepped off the plane from Rome—and in this case he actually had. They were at ease with one another, having been introduced years earlier, when Litvinenko had been working with an Italian governmental committee that had been investigating ex-FSB operatives supposedly involved in Italian politics. Even so, Mario had always struck Litvinenko as a man who *wanted* to be a spy, more than a man who actually was one. To Litvinenko, the Italian was a tourist in the gray edges where Litvinenko made his home—but he was eager, and it always seemed like he wanted to be helpful.

When he had first contacted Litvinenko this time around, asking to meet over a late lunch, Litvinenko had been skeptical. The man was often trying to arrange meetings to pass over information that was either not useful, or too subtle to be easily interpreted—and today, in particular, Litvinenko's day was a busy one. That very morning, just a few hours earlier, Litvinenko had met with contacts from Moscow at a nearby hotel to discuss a deal. One of the men—Andrei Lugovoy—was, coincidentally, a former ORT employee of Berezovsky—the same ex-FSB agent who had been briefly imprisoned after Glushkov's reported escape attempt in 2003.

The group of Russians was going to meet again that evening for drinks—which left little time for Litvinenko to complete the other errands he had in mind for that day. Fitting Mario in for a late lunch at the sushi joint was going to have him rushing all over the city— but then, at the last minute, he'd decided to give the Italian a little bit of his time.

In general, the years since Litvinenko had made London his home had been busy. Agitating, as his friend Berezovsky liked to say, was a full-time job. Litvinenko had written or cowritten a pair of books attacking Putin, had met numerous contacts among like-minded revolutionaries, and he always had his eyes open to try to find more ways to use his particular skills for profit or ex-pat politics. Like his patron, he had his fingers in many things, projects that came and went, most having to do with information, with navigating his way through the gray edge—or helping others navigate their way through the gray edge.

Whether it was a government, a corporation, or something else, Litvinenko knew that what he could provide would always have some value. The fact that sometimes he found himself working with individuals in less than "clean" fields . . . well, that just came with the territory.

Arms dealing, corporate espionage, political machinations, these intrigued him, and he often allowed himself to go a little too deep, to play out conspiracies in his mind—but he had witnessed enough real conspiracies to know that there were often elements of fact in the most surreal situations.

When Mario had told him that he had procured information that Litvinenko needed to see, it was too intriguing an offer to pass up. Even a would-be spy could stumble into something real once in a while.

But from the moment they had sat down in the sushi joint, Mario had sounded like a busted record, telling Litvinenko that both their lives were in danger from Russian hitmen. This was certainly not new information; Litvinenko was well aware that many members of the FSB thought of him as a traitor. He was convinced that Putin had seen his actions as an ultimate, almost incomprehensible betrayal. Likewise, Litvinenko had pushed the entire agency's buttons by his whistle-blowing, and his actions since he had come to London hadn't helped matters at all. He had made many open accusations against the FSB and Putin personally, even once going so far as to call the president a pedophile.

Litvinenko would've been surprised if there *weren't* people in Russia who wanted to do him harm. In fact, he had even been told by contacts that at least one FSB training group was using a photo of him on their rifle range, as a target.

"If you came to London to warn me about my former agency," Litvinenko said, stabbing at the pieces of sushi on the table in front of him with a chopstick, "you could've put it in a postcard."

The Italian smiled, then shook his head.

"Don't confuse the appetizer with the main course," he said, trying his best to sound dramatic.

He pulled a packet of papers out from under his coat. Then he tossed them across the small table, and waited as Litvinenko looked through the first few paragraphs.

Litvinenko finally raised his eyebrows.

"This is something, isn't it?"

Mario held his hands up in front of him.

"Not something you would want to put in a postcard, I think."

Litvinenko reread the paragraphs, then continued on through the document. The sounds of the sushi bar—the clatter of chopsticks, the conversations of other diners—receded.

The papers had to do with a case Litvinenko had been extremely focused on in the past few weeks. A murder, of course—these things always tended to revolve around a murder. This time, it had been the gunning down of a well-known journalist in Moscow who had made a name for herself through her opposition to the Kremlin. One month ago, she had been assassinated, shot four times at close range in an elevator in her apartment building, the pistol left right beside her dead body.

The papers that Mario had just handed him might very well provide a clue to the situation. Not a smoking gun perhaps but a link Litvinenko might be able to follow further.

To many, Litvinenko was nothing but a rabid conspiracy theorist. The books he had written had been dismissed by many as being similar to the sort of crap 9/11 deniers had put out in America, even years after the terrorist attack. But Litvinenko didn't care what people thought of him. He lived in a world of conspiracies and, often, the imagined were much tamer than the real.

He put the papers in his jacket and quickly rose from the table. He needed to make copies of them immediately, and he also wanted to show them to the one person with an imagination even more vivid than his own.

◆　◆　◆

The afternoon had dwindled away by the time Litvinenko was on his way toward the Mayfair hotel for his already arranged meeting with the Russians from the morning. It felt like his entire day—much of it in transit, by car, by foot, by bus—had him in a haze of jumbled, interlocking thoughts. He was still going over that morning meeting at the hotel, something that should have been the only thing occupying his mind. But the papers Mario had handed him vied for his brain's attention. The investigation into the journalist's murder in Moscow was a pet project that he felt certain would yield fruit, in his continued personal battle with his perceived nemesis—and perhaps the papers would lead him further on that quest.

Unfortunately, he hadn't been able to discuss anything with Berezovsky yet that day. His boss was going through many problems of his own. Though Berezovsky's lifestyle seemed as extravagant as ever, if not more so, in the past couple of years, rumor had it that the Oligarch's finances were not what they once had been. The Russian government had relentlessly gone after whatever properties and assets of his they could get to, and Berezovsky had made many investments that collapsed, and many more that didn't seem very profitable. His ex-wife Galina was gearing up for an epic divorce battle, which many in the UK believed could earn her hundreds of millions of dollars.

Berezovsky had also been pouring money into his quest to cause problems for Putin, funding any project that came to him that seemed like something to cause pain for the Russian government. From what Litvinenko had heard, the Oligarch had also been pushing his partner Badri more and more into Georgian politics, berating him, some would say, into sticking his neck out in the treacherous political landscape of the breakaway republic—even prodding him to run for president, a role the man didn't seem particularly suited to, given his calm, controlled, quiet demeanor, his penchant for staying out of the ᴄᴿamatic limelight and behind the scenes. As Berezovsky knew better than most, politics was an expensive hobby, and since he and Badri appeared to share elements of their bankroll, it was going to be another massive drain on the Oligarch's bottom line.

These growing financial issues would be particularly galling to Berezovsky, especially considering that just a year and a half earlier, Roman Abramovich, his continued obsession, had sold a controlling stake in Sibneft for what had been reported to be a valuation of eighteen billion dollars. The Oligarch had to watch how high his former protégé was rising, while he himself was still battling away in the same war that he'd been fighting for most of the decade.

In any event, Litvinenko needed to refocus again on his Russian contacts, the men he'd met earlier in the hotel in Soho. The afternoon was almost gone, so Litvinenko hurried his pace, already late for the rendezvous.

◆　◆　◆

Leather banquettes, dark wood tones, subtle lighting, an old-world bar that stretched along one wall from one end to the other, lit by the reflected glow of dozens of bottles of aging scotch, brandy, cognac, a veritable metropolis of liquor—the Pine Bar at the Millennium Hotel in Mayfair was much more Litvinenko's speed, he thought to himself as he followed Lugovoy out of the hotel lobby and into the dark atmosphere of the bar. The other two Russians were already at the table, drinks in front of them. Litvinenko took an empty seat between Lugovoy and the other man that he had met that morning at the hotel—another former agent, he believed, though he wasn't sure if he had ever met the man before that day. Lugovoy had already told them in the lobby that their meeting would be brief—really just a toast to their continued relationship, and the possibility that they would be working together in the future. The meeting had to be rushed because the other men were headed to a football game, at Emirates Stadium, which would already be filling up with the faithful. Funny, Litvinenko thought to himself, that Berezovsky would be at the same game, though Litvinenko didn't think there was any connection. These men still went back and forth to Moscow, and presumably were now in good graces with the government there. They had made their money and contacts, no doubt in the same gray edge where Litvinenko plied his trade.

The meeting did indeed go quickly; the conversation remained light and amiable, they didn't get too deep into business, and then Litvinenko was on his way. Because of the late hour, he had arranged a ride home with one of his closest friends in London, an exile—and former terrorist leader, according to the Kremlin—a man named Akhmed Zakayev.

Funny how life worked. In a former life, they had been on two sides locked in a battle marked by bombings, assassinations, murder. Now they were carpooling through the narrow streets of London.

CHAPTER THIRTY

November 2, 2006, 2 a.m.,

Muswell Hill, London

A FLECK OF SILVERY DUST, no bigger than a grain of sand, sus-
pended in a microscopic gel. Spinning, twirling, pirouetting within
a viscous bolus of saliva. Mouth, to pharynx, to esophagus, dragged
ever downward by the twin engines of muscle fiber and gravity. A
fleck, a tiny microgram of material that, in even smaller quantities,
existed all over nature—in plants and soil and even human cells—
but in this form, at this weight, could only have been created and
processed in a handful of highly sophisticated laboratories. A molecule, at this weight, was so incredibly rare that only three nations
had the ability to manufacture it. So spectacularly uncommon, it
wasn't discovered until the nineteenth century, by a woman made
famous by discovering rare and uncommon elements, who still had
found herself so intrigued by this particular particle, she'd named it
after the country of her birth.

A silvery, infinitesimally small flake, twisting, dancing, bouncing
against the esophageal walls—and as it went, spewing a constant
exhaust of even smaller flakes, that grew together into a billowing,

angry, atomic cloud: alpha particles, overexcited helium nuclei, obscenely swollen by a pair of neutrons and a pair of protons. Each too big and heavy to pass through anything thicker than a sheet of paper—and yet, within the confines of a human body, releasing a cloud of devastating power, anywhere from two hundred fifty thousand to a million times more deadly than hydrogen cyanide, destroying every cell it touched. First, the stratified squamous cells of the esophagus; the merest glance of the alpha particles turned these cells inside out, tearing through their fragile walls, causing them to implode. Then on down, into the stomach, spreading out across the mucosa and into the gastric pits; ripping into the individual cells and rending them apart, causing large gashes of inflammation, boring into each cell's center, bombarding the fragile DNA within until the strands weakened, bowed, then shattered.

On it went—through the dying stomach lining, through the ruptured intestinal walls, into the bloodstream, hijacking the platelets and white blood cells to traverse the highways and byways of the circulatory system, spreading to each and every organ, one by one: the kidneys, the liver, the spleen. Finding the lymphatic nodes, the lungs, the skin, the hair, the bone marrow, and eventually, the heart.

One fleck of silvery dust, churning like the meltdown of a nuclear reactor through the body of the man as he slept next to his ballroom dancer, in the quiet suburb of North London.

✦ ✦ ✦

Sometime between midnight and dawn, Litvinenko suddenly came awake, as a knifelike pain tore through his lower abdomen. He hunched forward into a fetal ball, then rolled carefully out of bed, trying not to wake Marina. They had gone to bed fairly late, having enjoyed their favorite meal together, a chicken dish he'd mastered as a bachelor during his agency training. It was a meal he could prepare in his sleep; he doubted he'd undercooked anything in a way that might be causing him such a fierce bout of gastric distress.

As he stumbled into the bathroom and leaned over the open toilet, his thoughts shifted through his day—the morning at the Soho hotel, the sushi bar on Piccadilly, Berezovsky's office, the Pine Bar at the Mayfair. Could it have been the sushi? He didn't drink alcohol, but he believed he'd had a sip of green tea with Lugovoy and the other Russians, really just to be polite. Hardly the sort of thing that could be causing the intense cramping and searing pain he was now experiencing.

He leaned forward, and it felt like his insides were coming out. Again and again, he retched into the toilet, until he could hear Marina stirring in the bedroom. *Food poisoning—it had to be.* Although he'd had food poisoning before, he didn't remember it feeling this severe. It was like being on fire on the inside, a bizarre, unsettling sensation. He retched again, the muscles of his stomach snarling into a vicious knot beneath his skin. An awful, horrible feeling; but he reminded himself he'd been through worse. Hell, he'd spent most of a year in one of the most soul-crushing prisons in the world. He could handle a piece of bad sushi.

"Are you okay, Sasha?" he heard from the bedroom.

He coughed up a speck of bile, then exhaled, forcing a smile.

"I'll live. But I might be in here a while."

Then his stomach convulsed again, and he leaned back over the toilet, his insides still swirling with that strange intensity, the likes of which he'd never felt before.

CHAPTER THIRTY-ONE

November 23, 2006, 9:21 p.m.

University College Hospital, London, Quarantine Unit, ICU

WHEN ALEXANDER LITVINENKO'S HEART seized for the final time, ending three devastating weeks of a slow, horrific deterioration, he was certain he knew why he was about to die, and believed he finally understood what was about to kill him, even though the exact sequence of events that had led to his death would remain one of the greatest stories of the decade.

Although he had been first admitted to Barnet General Hospital in London on November 4, two days after he'd fallen ill, it wasn't until a week later that doctors began to suspect he'd been poisoned. By November 13, specialists had tested samples of his urine, blood, hair, and skin, and were convinced he was suffering from an immense dose of thallium—a tasteless, odorless heavy metal, deadly in even small doses—but sometimes treatable, if discovered soon enough. He was immediately given the antidote—Prussian blue, a synthetic pigment used in certain paints, that also had the unique property of being able to trap thallium in the small intestine, limiting the amount of damage it could do to the human body.

Two days later, despite the Prussian blue, Litvinenko was in critical condition. His formerly athletic body had become nearly skeletal, his hair had fallen out, he was unable to stand, and he was in such pain that he was unable to swallow or take any food. On November 17, he was moved to University College Hospital, and a major police investigation began; specialists from all over Britain were called in, and tissue, urine, and blood samples were sent to labs all over the world. Three days later, he was placed in intensive care, and his gathered friends, family, and colleagues distributed photos of him—his decimated, bedridden form, barely more than a corpse—to the international press.

It wasn't until yesterday, November 22, that his samples had finally made their way to the British Atomic Weapons Establishment—a military lab specializing in combating nuclear terrorism. Twenty four hours later—at 7:30 p.m. on the 23rd, less than two hours ago—the true method of poisoning had finally been discovered: polonium 210—a radioactive material, that, though found in minute amounts in nature, could not be manufactured in significant amounts except with the use of a nuclear reactor.

The implications of such a bizarre murder weapon were immense and made Litvinenko instantly famous, perhaps the first case of nuclear assassination. Strange, he might have thought to himself, had his body and brain not been racked by the horrors of an internal atomic meltdown, how a bit player, a member of the chorus, had suddenly exploded into the forefront, not through anything he'd done in life, but in the way he was going to die.

As Scotland Yard's investigation went into full swing—a high-tech mouse hunt involving dozens of police officers, scientists, and antiterrorism agents. It became instantly evident that the method of the murder, though probably designed to be a silent, unstoppable killer, since polonium 210 is an isotope with a half-life that should have been short enough for all traces to disappear from Litvinenko's body within a month's time—would also yield clues backward, maybe to the killers themselves—because the dose had been so great, the material so difficult to control, and the effects so sudden, that the trail of radiation would likely be detectable—maybe even all the way back to its source.

The minute the specialists, garbed in protective suits, their radiation detection equipment at the ready, began following Litvinenko's reconstructed movements of the day before he'd first become ill—November 1—they'd discovered an incredible road map of varyingly powerful alpha particles running like glowing silver veins across the city of London—and beyond. Beginning at the Pine Bar, where seven employees of the hotel would test positive for polonium, to the seat where Litvinenko had been sitting, even to the painting that had hung behind him on the wall—and from there, backward. Polonium had been found in the bus he had taken that day, as well as at 7 Down Street, in Berezovksy's office. Traces had been found in the sushi bar on Piccadilly, in the hotel room where he had met Lugovoy that morning. Then even further back, to multiple cities across Europe, as well as on two British Airways flights. The trail went cold, as the investigators followed it back to Moscow, where the Russian authorities shut them down, insisting that the plot had more to do with British Intelligence, which they believed had their own connections with Litvinenko and a reason to smear the Russian state, than with a pair of former FSB agents who were involved in the dark goings-on in Litvinenko's shadowy world.

In the end, as the investigation moved toward an international standoff that would still rage on years later, Litvinenko was forced to resolve himself to focus on the things he felt sure of rather than the things that might forever remain a mystery.

To that end, before he was too weak to communicate, he made a final, deathbed statement, to tell the world exactly what he believed had happened, at whose orders, and why. And then he said good-bye to his wife the ballroom dancer, told her he loved her, and closed his eyes.

◆   ◆   ◆

On November 24, 2006, Alex Goldfarb, a friend and colleague of Litvinenko, who had helped him emigrate to London, and also a close associate of Boris Berezovsky, stood outside the front entrance of University College Hospital, and read Litvinenko's final statement. After thanking the British police, the British government, and the British people, and reiterating his love for his wife and son, the words turned immediately dark—dipping deep into the shadows where he had made his home:

"As I lie here I can distinctly hear the beating of wings of the angel of death. I may be able to give him the slip, but I have to say my legs do not run as fast as I would like. I think, therefore, that this may be the time to say one or two things to the person responsible for my present condition. You may succeed in silencing me, but that silence comes at a price. You have shown yourself to be as barbaric and ruthless as your most hostile critics have claimed. You have shown yourself to have no respect for life, liberty, or any civilized value. You have shown yourself to be unworthy of your office, to be unworthy of the trust of civilized men and women. You may succeed in silencing one man—but the howl of protest from around the world will reverberate, Mr. Putin, in your ears for the rest of your life."

CHAPTER THIRTY-TWO

December 1, 2006,

Highgate Cemetery, London

THE RAIN WAS COMING down in sheets, gusts of icy wind swirling between the high metal bars of the gates leading into the ancient cemetery—but still Berezovsky found himself lingering just outside the entrance, mostly hidden in the shadows of the oversize umbrella held low above his head by his Israeli bodyguard. His eyes burned from too many tears shed over the past few hours; the short ceremony at Regent's Park Mosque, earlier that day, had been a sad, if confusing, affair. There was some dispute as to whether the ceremony should have taken place in a mosque at all. Whether Litvinenko had actually converted to Islam before his death, as some close to him contended, or whether he was simply voicing his solidarity with the Chechens, whom he considered his allies in his consuming battle with the Russian government, was the subject of some dispute. To add further complications, the mosque had refused to allow the dead ex-agent's body to be brought inside, because of the danger of radioactive contamination.

Everything about the murder, the tragic, torturous death, even this funeral—at the same cemetery where Karl Marx was buried, attended by a crowd that included a former separatist leader, a handful of ex-FSB agents, agitators of all stripes and colors—seemed simply incredible. When Berezovsky had learned the method of the young man's death—polonium poisoning?—he was shocked. Such an unbelievable way to kill someone. Perhaps it had really been Lugovoy and the other Russian, who were now back in Moscow, denying any involvement—and in fact, facing their own health battles from radioactive poisoning, whether as a result of being near Litvinenko when he was poisoned—or because they themselves had indeed been involved in the poisoning. There was always the possibility that perhaps some other contact or enemy of Litvinenko had done it, since, to be fair, the man lived in a world full of dangerous men, brimming with rogue agents, counterspies, Mafia figures, arms dealers, God knew who else. Whoever was responsible, it was a terrifying act.

As the investigation grew more heated, day by day, Berezovksy had told the officers from Scotland Yard who interrogated him that he didn't know who had killed his young friend. Though Litvinenko's statement had made it clear who he had thought was to blame, there were almost too many potential suspects. Even Berezovksy himself had come under suspicion, because of the traces of polonium found in his office.

Of course, he had denied any involvement. But even though he'd reluctantly let the officers question him and search 7 Down Street, he hadn't spoken to the press at all—keeping uncharacteristically silent. The truth was, this murder had come at a difficult and chaotic moment in his life. His financial issues were growing, but despite that, he was spending like a man with a limitless supply. He had also spent enormous sums of money and long periods of time in planning and supporting Badri's growing role in Georgian politics—despite his friend's reluctance. Really, Badri was a brother in Berezovsky's eyes; they had grown so close over the years. Although Badri seemed more interested in repairing their relationship with Putin and Russia's government, and finding a status quo that didn't involve them constantly being surrounded by bodyguards, Berezovsky had refused to let the man rest on his laurels, watching as their enemies continued to flourish.

Like Roman Abramovich, Berezovsky thought to himself, as the wind kicked a spray of thick droplets across his cheeks, which seemed to be growing more sallow every passing day. His former subordinate had risen to incredible heights, after selling a controlling portion of Sibneft for thirteen billion dollars, making him one of the richest men in the world—and perhaps the richest man in Russia. The number was *ten* times what Abramovich had paid Berezovsky and Badri at the Megève heliport. If they had split the company down the middle, Berezovsky would have received another five billion dollars—perhaps more. With that kind of money, he could have funded a dozen revolutions against Putin—and still had money left over to pay for his upcoming divorce.

Of course, staring through those cemetery gates, it seemed inappropriate to be thinking about money, even if the numbers ran into the billions. It all seemed so unimportant, next to the murder of the young agent.

Then again, whoever had killed Litvinenko had certainly managed to elevate the young agent in a way he had never been able to achieve himself. In death, he'd become a much bigger agitation than he'd ever been in life. In fact, in many ways, he was a bigger story than Berezovsky himself.

It was not lost on Berezovksy that the cameras lined up just beyond the police cordon, not twenty yards from where he was standing, were a legion beyond any he had ever managed to gather on his own. Not just press from Britain and Russia, but from every country in the world.

Litvinenko had lived in the shadows, but now, in his death, the lights of those cameras were blasting through, like spotlights across a black stage, searching for the lead actor.

What Berezovsky really needed, more than money, he realized, was a way to step into those spotlights. To do something spectacular enough, dramatic enough, to catch the world's attention once and for all.

CHAPTER THIRTY-THREE

October 5, 2007,

Hermès store, 179 Sloane Street, London

TEN MONTHS OF PLANNING, ten months of late-night strategy sessions, minute calculations, collected flight plans, train schedules, reports from private eyes and contacts in cities all over the world, and when Berezovsky finally pulled it off, when he finally succeeded, it wasn't the result of some brilliant machinations on his part, it was simply an accident of chance. When he had left his home that afternoon, he had only been on his way to buy a shirt.

Even that first effort had ended in failure. Berezovksy had been leaving the Dolce & Gabbana store on Sloane Street, a dejected look on his face, because he hadn't found anything that fit properly. He had lost a fair amount of weight in the past few months, due to his worsening credit issues. To be fair, he was still very rich; his armored Maybach was parked just a few feet from the posh store, right at the curb, engines running, his driver and bodyguard waiting for him outside. But he was definitely in the kind of mood that called for a little designer-brand therapy, and he felt sure a new five hundred dollar shirt would have raised his spirits.

But as soon as he had stepped out of the fancy clothing shop, and saw the way his driver was pointing excitedly down the block, he realized that perhaps a new shirt would be a tiny victory, compared to what was about to happen.

"He's right there," his driver shouted, loud enough for Berezovksy to hear from across the sidewalk. "At Hermès. Two doors down."

Berezovsky followed the man's extended finger, peering down the crowded sidewalk, filled with well-heeled Friday afternoon shoppers. Almost instantly, he saw a spectacular sight. The team of professional-looking bodyguards would have been impossible to miss, even for a man not as well versed in the security efforts of the exceedingly wealthy as Berezovsky was. He recognized at least one of the three bodyguards immediately, and that was all he needed; this was truly the moment he had been waiting for.

"Get the documents!" he shouted to his driver.

He watched as the man leapt back into the car, quickly retrieving a sealed manila envelope. Then Berezovsky gestured with his hand, indicating for the rest of his team to come out of the car and join them on the sidewalk. As usual, he had his full complement of security with him, now mostly Israeli, well trained, and inconspicuously armed. They contracted around him, creating a phalanx that protected him from all sides, and together, the team moved down the crowded sidewalk toward the Hermès store. Passersby stopped and stared, but also quickly got out of the way, as the lead bodyguard hurried his pace.

Berezovsky remained in the center of the men, his small form obscured by their much larger presence, until the group reached the front of the Hermès store, pulling to a stop right next to the large, plate-glass window, which separated the bustling sidewalk from the elegant display shelves containing tens of thousands of dollars' worth of purses, wallets, and scarves. As soon as Berezovksy's team arrived, the other group of bodyguards closed ranks in front of the doorway, blocking the entrance. Berezovksy could see the fear on their faces. Even though they couldn't see him yet, they knew exactly who they were facing. And, no doubt, they had been given direct orders not to let him pass.

"This is illegal!" Berezovsky shouted. "I have a right to shop wherever I want."

He took the manila envelope from his driver, who was standing close to him, and then stepped back, as his team of bodyguards advanced. Suddenly, a small scuffle erupted as the two groups of men began pushing and shoving each other. As they battled, Berezovsky waited for an opening. When one of his men pushed one of the opposing men back, a space was revealed, just big enough for a pint-size Oligarch.

Berezovksy took the opportunity and sprinted forward, sliding between the two bodyguards and through the doorway into the elegant shop.

The store went instantly silent, as the shoppers inside stared in awe at the spectacle out front. But Berezovksy didn't care about the tourists, store clerks, and Londoners. He scanned the floor with quick flicks of his eyes—and saw his quarry right up front, trying to look inconspicuous. Berezovksy rushed toward him, and didn't stop moving until he was less than a foot away.

Roman Abramovich stared down at him. Berezovksy, in turn, smiled sweetly—and suddenly showed Abramovich the manila envelope.

"I have a present for you," he said.

Berezovsky tossed the envelope toward Abramovich's hands;

the envelope missed the younger man's fingers, then fluttered to the floor.

But Berezovsky had already turned on his heels, and was heading back out the front door of the shop. He shouted at his driver to get the car, and the jostling swarm of bodyguards separated.

A moment later, Berezovsky was back in the quiet confines of his Maybach.

For nearly six months, he had kept that manila envelope close, as he had chased Abramovich all around the country. He had even once shown up at a Chelsea Football Club match, but had been unable to force his way past Abramovich's security to the owner's box. And now, entirely by coincidence, he had been shopping two doors down from the man.

It had taken one giant happy coincidence, but now Berezovsky had officially served Abramovich. When his former protégé finally opened the envelope and looked inside, he would see the most historic papers in modern English legal times. *The largest civil lawsuit in recorded history.*

Boris Berezovsky was suing his former protégé for five billion, six hundred million dollars, claiming that the young man had forced him to sell both his television station and his oil interests at unfair prices, through coercion and blackmail.

A part of Berezovsky believed that Abramovich would never let such a thing go to trial. The man had become well known in the British press for being averse to all forms of public attention. He barely spoke in the open, and kept his life as hidden as possible. Berezovsky believed that Abramovich would probably settle, pay him a large sum of money to keep this out of a courtroom.

If he didn't, well, Berezovksy *wanted* everything to come out in the open. Every step he had taken, everything he had done, in business politics—everything that had happened over the past decade, and more.

All of it out in the open, in a courtroom in front of the cameras of the world.

There would be risks involved, for sure. The story had many dark angles, and Berezovsky had no idea how he was going to look when it was all laid bare. Badri had not wanted him to take such a bold step, had in fact warned that it was crazy and that he should let things be. But, in the end, although Badri would not be involved in the suit, he had agreed to be a supporting witness.

Berezovsky wasn't concerned with what Badri thought or even what Abramovich might think. What mattered, to him, was that once again, he would be important—and the entire world would be watching.

CHAPTER THIRTY-FOUR

February 12, 2008,

Downside Manor, Surrey, England

WHEN THE PHONE RANG at two in the morning in Berezovksy's bedroom at his estate in a posh suburb of London—waking him from a deep sleep—and he pressed the receiver to his ear to listen to the grief-stricken voice on the other end, he knew in an instant that his fortunes had yet again changed for the worse. Before any discussions of any potential settlement in his historic lawsuit, years before anyone would set foot in a courtroom—any excitement or optimism Berezovsky had felt in the wake of that wonderful Friday afternoon four months earlier, vanished in a stroke of completely unexpected news.

Five minutes later, Berezovsky was in the back of his car, still finishing with the buttons of his coat. His driver tore through the countryside of wealthy estates, on the short trip to Downside Manor, one of the most elegant mansions in Surrey. But even as Berezovsky's car skidded up the long driveway to the main house, he could see that the police had already set up their cordon, stringing their damn yellow tape all the way around the manicured lawn, blocking off access to the home itself.

For once, Berezovksy was out of his car before his bodyguards; he rushed straight toward the nearest constable and began shouting at the man to let him through. Berezovsky wasn't even sure what he was saying, whether he was speaking Russian or English—by this point, the tears were streaming freely down his face. But the policeman blocked his way, refusing to let him pass.

The officer obviously didn't understand. Though they didn't share the same last name, Berezovsky and Badri were more than brothers. For nearly two decades, they had been in contact nearly every day, had lived like members of the same family, and had built a relationship well beyond friendship. From the very first days at the car company, Badri had been his right hand.

And now the Georgian was gone. Fifty-two years old, he had succumbed to a sudden heart attack, having dropped to the floor in his bedroom just a few hours ago.

Berezovsky's shoulders slumped as he stood in the driveway, as one of his bodyguards tried to explain the situation to the constable. In truth, it didn't really matter. Badri's widow had told Berezovksy all he needed to know. The coroner had already declared him dead—and the police were already beginning their investigation.

Of course, there would be suspicions. Badri was living in exile, and was also the richest man in Georgia.

A month earlier, he had been a candidate for president of the breakaway nation, a campaign that had ended in pure catastrophe. In December, during the heated political process, the opposition had given the press a tape recorded in this very mansion, evidence that implicated Badri in a scandal that involved his attempts to bribe a high-level Georgian minister to help him defeat the very same pro-Western candidate that he and Berezovsky had previously put into office during the Rose Revolution.

Berezovksy had never doubted the veracity of the tape. Such a bribe seemed like business as usual where they came from, and in their history. But the incident had completely destroyed Badri's chances, and in the following election, he had received less than ten percent of the vote.

The loss had been hard on Badri; the impropriety of what he had done had made him look corrupt, and had ruined his reputation in the place he was most beloved.

Perhaps that had been part of what had led him to such an early grave. Berezovksy understood the impact that failure could have on a man like Badri. A billionaire could feel depressed as easily as a pauper.

For certain, Berezovsky believed that Badri had been going through some sort of emotional crisis. Badri had even suggested that he and Berezovsky should reassess their financial arrangements, pulling himself free of what had been a long-term, unwritten sharing of a bankroll. Berezovsky wondered if Badri's request was a response to feeling that he had been pushed into politics.

But none of that mattered now. Berezovksy couldn't believe his friend had died. Berezovksy had always assumed that he would be the one to go first.

Standing in the darkness, looking up at the lavish mansion from behind the police tape, he felt more alone than ever before. At the same time, he felt a twinge of fear, as he began to wonder how much further his fortunes could fall.

CHAPTER THIRTY-FIVE

October 3, 2011,

High Court, The Rolls Building, Fetter Lane, London

IF PURE SPECTACLE HAD been Berezovsky's only goal—and even he would admit that spectacle in itself had always been something he'd strived for—from the very first moment of what the press was calling a historic showdown between Oligarchs, he was succeeding on every cylinder. Sitting in the back of his Maybach, watching as the phalanx of reporters from all over the world convulsed around Abramovich and his fashion-plate significant other heading into the modern, glass-and-steel court complex, he felt an intense satisfaction. He could tell, just from the look on Abramovich's face, that the attention was sheer torture for the normally sheltered man. And this walk through the barrage of press—something that would no doubt become a morning ritual over the many months of the upcoming trial—was just the tip of the iceberg. The British newspapers, television tabloids, and talk show hosts had become obsessed with "The Biggest Trial in History"—and plenty of their passion and titillation had been focused on the extreme details of Abramovich's wealth. His reported twelve-billion-dollar fortune, his soccer team, his airplanes, his homes, his newest yacht—the Eclipse, the biggest in the world, with multiple helipads, swimming pools, Picassos on the walls.

For a private man who rarely spoke in public, never gave interviews, and kept counsel with a very few close friends and confidants—a life lived from behind gates and a veritable army of bodyguards—the attention had to seem like a form of persecution. Berezovsky was still somewhat shocked that Abramovich had let this go to trial, that he was going to sit there, in that brand-new courtroom, and lay open much of his life in such a fishbowl setting. The state-of-the-art justice complex, a bulbous, space-age building filled with open atria, spiral staircases, and lofty ceilings—had just been completed. Yet it seemed a strangely anachronistic place in which to debate a case lodged squarely in a moment in Russian history. Then again, the case did hinge around a sudden, spontaneous modernization, a revolution of market forces, the decline of an old way and the rising up of something new. Perhaps glass and steel made more sense than aging stone.

Whatever the location, Berezovsky felt that, at least here, in the moment before the trial began, he had achieved a victory; he had spent his whole life on a quest to be at the center of things. Here and now, he would have his chance to tell his story in front of the entire world. Whether it was arrogance, confidence, or even maybe a bit of delusion, he was certain the world would be sympathetic.

He waited until Abramovich had entered the building, then just a little longer for the press to settle back, recharge their camera batteries, restock their audio recorders. And then he signaled to his driver and bodyguards. He was ready for it to begin.

◆　◆　◆

Courtroom 26 wasn't large; a rectangular box set up so that everything faced the judge's bench, a space barely big enough to accommodate the two teams of lawyers, bodyguards, and experts, with just a few rows for the registered press. Berezovsky had been placed fairly close to the entrance, which meant that every morning, Abramovich and his team would pass right by him on their way to their seats. He did his best not to have any contact with the other side—no words, not even looks—as they went by, on orders from his legal team. At each day's recess, the two sides were led to different holding rooms, an attempt to limit any incidental contact that could turn this into more of a circus than it already was.

From the very opening statements, it became clear how the trial was going to be presented. Berezovsky's argument was simple: Abramovich had been his protégé, his close friend, and someone he'd considered like a son. He'd made a deal to build an oil and aluminum empire with the young man, and although nothing had ever been written down, they had agreed to split the ownership of their business down the middle: fifty percent for Abramovich, fifty percent to Berezovsky and Badri. When Berezovsky had fallen out with Putin—a fact that was shared ground in their arguments—and had been forced to flee Russia, Abramovich had chosen to end their partnership. He'd used the pressure Berezovsky was under from Putin's regime to force the sale of Berezovksy's shares of ORT and his interest in Sibneft and the aluminum conglomerate—now known as Rusal—at fire-sale prices. In fact, Berezovsky further argued, Abramovich had used threats and blackmail to get a price that was almost one fifth of what Berezovsky felt his interests were worth.

For his part, Abramovich's argument was equally simple. In his view, there had never been any written agreement because there never was any deal of the sort Berezovsky had described between them. Berezovsky had never owned any shares of Sibneft or Rusal. And in fact, their relationship, from his point of view, wasn't at all the friendship that Berezovsky had described—it was actually an unwritten partnership between a young man and his krysha. In many ways, Abramovich's entire case revolved around this Russian concept, something his lawyer argued that a Western judge would have to go back to Shakespearean times to truly empathize with and understand. Abramovich hadn't paid Berezovsky and Badri one billion, three hundred million dollars in Megève because of a friendship or to buy any shares that didn't exist. He had paid that money to complete his krysha obligations.

Although the two sides' arguments hinged on fairly simple concepts, it was also obvious from the beginning that everything else about the case was going to be as complex as a spider web. A story spanning two decades, involving two men who had ridden through the chaos of that historic time in Russian history. A tale that ran from glasnost to perestroika to Yeltsin to Putin, that involved murders, arrests, an upheaval both political and economic, and of course enormous sums of money. Even though it had come from the opposing lawyer, Berezovksy had to agree that Shakespeare was an apt comparison. The judge, the Right Honorable Dame Elizabeth Gloster, was about to be thrown into a sweeping drama; it would be up to her to determine which of the players were honest, which were star-crossed and tragic—and which might be simply playing the fool.

CHAPTER THIRTY-SIX

August 31, 2012,

High Court, The Rolls Building

*N*INE MONTHS.

Early mornings in heated discussion with lawyers, consultants, family, his girlfriend; going over the testimony of the day before and what was still ahead. Then that mad dash through the swarming press—the flashbulbs going off, the microphones waving toward him like reeds in a heavy wind, the television cameras catching his every grin, every outfit, whether a shirt button was done or undone, whether he wore a flower in his lapel or a tie that seemed too colorful, whether Yelena had a scowl or a smile. Then the awkward moment when he and his opponent passed in the narrow aisle that led to each of their seats, the two teams of bodyguards sifting through each other in some sort of intricate puzzle of oversize muscles and ill-fitting suits. Once or twice, on the way to the bathroom, words might be spoken; but overall, the courtroom was a place of quiet professionalism.

Nine months.

Two very different men, two very different Oligarchs, taking the stand in between the cavalcade of witnesses, experts, employees, and hangers-on. Abramovich, always soft-spoken, always through a translator. A businessman, with a businessman's efficiency of word and concept, detailing the decisions he had made, and why he had made them. Describing himself as a man who wanted to be honest and open, caught in a world that was corrupt and chaotic. There was no hiding his ambition, the fact that he had done whatever was necessary to build his empire. But it seemed an almost emotionless ambition; he had seen Berezovsky as a necessary tool, a lever to wrest the oil business from the government, a connection that would keep him and his business safe. Berezovsky, in Abramovich's description, sounding like a gangster, who, along with his strongman Badri Patarkatsishvili, had been necessary to help him navigate the dangerous waters of a Mafia-like corporate and political atmosphere.

Berezovsky knew, as he took the stand, that he would appear to be Abramovich's polar opposite. Hitting his notes like a performer, raising his voice, nearing tears, always frenetic, often almost unhinged. Speaking in clipped English with his heavy Russian accent—and often contradicting himself—he overflowed with emotion, much of it directed at his former partner. He took great relish in calling his former protégé naive and stupid—although when he described their meeting on Pyotr Aven's yacht, he had to admit he'd found the young man's creativity inspiring. As the story progressed, as their relationship shifted on its axis, he again and again tried to hammer home the idea that Abramovich had gone from obsequious and helpless to threatening and dangerous. His accusations—mainly, that Abramovich had used the arrest of Glushkov and the threats coming from Putin as blackmail tools to get Berezovsky to part with ORT and his ownership of Sibneft—were couched as a personal affront, a betrayal from a young man Berezovsky had considered family. Abramovich had turned his back on a friend, a father, and had sided with a tyrant.

Nine months.

Back and forth they went, sifting through the stories of their parallel rise. Listening to the stories, retold in their own words and through numerous witnesses—everyone from Abramovich's cook, who had been on that helipad in Megève, to an esteemed professor of Russian history, whom Berezovsky had called on to explain the Yeltsin regime in the context of the fall of the Soviet regime—often filled Berezovsky with sadness. That same loneliness he had felt outside of Badri's home the night of his death plagued him; the Georgian's missing presence tore at him, especially when his friend's deposition—taken in the months before he died—was read aloud in the courtroom. Even when it diverged from Berezovsky's own memories, it took Berezovksy back to a time when everything seemed possible, when he was important—when he truly was at the center of it all.

Nine months.

And yet, as the trial moved through the decades, time traveling from point to point in the timeline, cherry-picking the intense, sometimes surreal, sometimes even comical moments that best illustrated the two opposing points of view, Berezovsky began to notice, more and more, that the stories—which were gleefully picked up by the press, fresh carrion laid out for gorging vultures—weren't painting him as important, but rather, as ludicrous. One story revolved around a meeting at the Dorchester Hotel in March of 2000, attended by Berezovsky, Badri, Roman, Eugene, and aluminum magnate Oleg Deripaska. There, Berezovsky claimed, a deal was struck outlining his ownership in their combined aluminum company, which he believed should have held under English law—but this argument was overshadowed by the salacious detail that Berezovsky, according to Deripaska, had apparently shown up for the meeting in his bathrobe, and by Deripaska's denial that any deal took place at all. At another point in the trial, Berezovsky inadvertently mentioned that he had offered some of his called witnesses one percent of whatever he won in the case—a comment he quickly tried to take back. And in another line of questioning, he told the court that he'd purchased a secretly taped conversation between himself, Abramovich, and Badri for fifty million dollars; but when questioned again about the tape, he explained that he hadn't had the fifty million dollars available, so instead he'd given his source a yacht.

Worse than being called a gangster by Abramovich's side, more and more he was being made to look the fool. Instead of the gravitas he'd hoped to achieve, he felt himself being mocked. When a text he'd sent to an associate was offered into evidence—supposedly signed "Dr. Evil"—he could see the opposing side's plan for what it was: an effort to make him appear like some sort of outdated godfather figure, an absurd mobster who had already been paid billions in what was essentially a protection racket.

In the end, Berezovsky tried to convince himself that the judge would see through these machinations. He had played a significant part in Russian history. He had put two presidents into the Kremlin, and he deserved respect—and a much larger piece of Abramovich's billions. If Badri had been next to him in that courtroom, his friend would have calmed his fears, played the part of anchor, as usual, and kept him from coming even more unhinged. But Badri wasn't there; Berezovsky was forced to rely on his legal team, his girlfriend, and his experts. He truly hoped it would be enough.

Hell, nine months was time enough to turn a single cell into a human life. It was certainly time enough for an English judge to understand the importance of a man like Boris Berezovsky.

◆ ◆ ◆

When the moment finally came, Berezovsky did his best to control his expression as he stared intently at the judge. He was trying to read her face, trying to see through the curvature of her eyes as she read through her notes at her bench, to the intent inside, trying to prepare himself for whatever verdict she gave. In his heart he believed she had only one choice: she had heard his story and now she was going to give him what was rightfully his—money, but also validation. The trial had laid bare the corruption of modern Russia, and the uniqueness of the Russian business environment. It had shown the world that a man from nothing, from nowhere, had used his brilliance and innate talents to build himself into the ultimate power broker—and how it had viciously been taken away by a tyrant and a former protégé, a former friend.

When the judge finally raised her eyes, a hush swept through Courtroom 26, and Berezovsky leaned forward in his seat, his heart pounding in his chest. She began to speak, legalese, first, English words that might as well have been Martian. Berezovsky found himself smiling; he could see, out of the corners of his eyes, both his team and Abramovich's team looking around at each other—everyone but the lawyers, who understood what was happening—but he kept his attention focused on the judge. Eventually, she began to make sense, her words shifting to something he could comprehend—and suddenly his entire face froze, the smile still in place, but behind it, only pain.

"On my analysis of the entirety of the evidence," she said, "I found Mr. Berezovsky an unimpressive and inherently unreliable witness, who regarded truth as a transitory, flexible concept, which could be molded to suit his current purposes. At times the evidence which he gave was deliberately dishonest; sometimes he was clearly making his evidence up as he went along . . . at other times, I gained the impression that he was not necessarily being deliberately dishonest, but had deluded himself into believing his own version of events. I regret to say that the bottom line of my analysis of Mr. Berezovsky's credibility is that he would have said almost anything to support his case."

From there, she continued to the details of the case. For twenty minutes, maybe more, she spoke, but Berezovksy was already gone, his mind swirling away from that courtroom, away from the pain of what he considered a personal attack on his character, on his memory, on his life. Abramovich had won the trial, that was obvious. But it was almost irrelevant. The judgment was not only about billions—money that Berezovsky desperately needed to support his lifestyle—but about how the world would see him from this point on. *Dishonest, unreliable, a gangster, a liar.*

Worst of all, the word that struck him like a blow to his very soul: *unimpressive.*

As the judge finally finished speaking, as Courtroom 26 began to clear, Berezovsky remained still as stone, rooted to his seat.

It was clear to him now. He had truly lost everything.

CHAPTER THIRTY-SEVEN

March 22, 2013,

Four Seasons Hotel, Park Lane, London

FROM WHERE BEREZOVSKY WAS standing, in a darkened corner at the very end of the long, black-lacquered bar, half leaning against the edge of a chest-high chair paneled in a deep crimson velvet, he could just make out the pianist's fingers as they trickled along the ivory keys, following the pattern of notes behind a tune decidedly jazzy in nature, something Western and light and airy, but still with a hint of depth, lilting scales that went on forever, rising above the noise in the crowded, elegant lounge, above the clink of glasses and the clang of silverware, of couples chatting, businessmen discussing deals, tourists consulting maps and considering museums, churches, restaurants. Music that should have been nothing but background, somehow elevated to the point where it was all Berezovsky could hear.

He wasn't certain why he was still in the bar. The Four Seasons was quite close to his office, easily within walking distance; even so, of course his car was waiting outside, engine running. He could also have headed home, to his mansion in the suburbs, or perhaps to the flat he kept in the city. He could have headed out of London, to any number of places. Well, any number of places that didn't have any sort of extradition treaties with Russia, that weren't in the midst of the relentless machine gobbling up more of his assets, confiscating his houses or boats or cars.

But the engine that had powered him for so long—the adrenaline that had kept him running at such incredible speed, rushing from one thing to another, a bullet train, a man who couldn't keep still within his own skin—had finally seized, shut down, gone cold. And here he was, standing in a bar just a few blocks from his office, thinking through the short interview he had just given moments before.

It had been the first time he'd spoken to anyone in the press since the trial. In fact, he'd essentially hidden himself away for the past seven months, since that horrifying verdict, refusing most visitors, not answering any mail, even changing his phone number. He wasn't sure why he had finally relented. Maybe he'd realized that at the very least, he needed to try to put his thoughts out loud; maybe, somehow, speaking would organize the swirling chaos that now dominated his mind.

The reporter, a native Russian, a competent, intelligent journalist by the name of Ilya Zhegulev—had, ironically, been from the Russian edition of *Forbes*—the same magazine Berezovsky had sued for libel for suggesting that he was some sort of gangster. Since then, Paul Klebnikov, the journalist who wrote that piece—and coined the label "Godfather of the Kremlin"—had been gunned down outside the *Forbes* office in Moscow. On July 9, 2004, he'd been shot nine times with a semiautomatic pistol, then taken to a nearby hospital in an ambulance that didn't have any functioning oxygen tanks—only to bleed to death in an elevator that had somehow become stuck for over fifteen minutes in the hospital basement. Klebnikov's murder remained unsolved, even though many fingers had pointed at Berezovsky.

But Berezovsky was beyond caring about irony; he wasn't sure what had made him finally acquiesce to speak with the Russian writer—and, in retrospect, going back over what he had said, he knew that it would have taken more than a quality journalist or an experienced linguist to decipher what he'd been trying to say. From the very beginning, he'd realized that maybe he'd been wrong to think he was ready to make any sort of statement. Throughout the interview, he'd continually asked that it be off the record.

If he remembered the conversation correctly, he'd started off by both attacking and praising Badri; trying to explain recent press reports that he and Badri had gone through some sort of financial "divorce" before Badri passed away, which had resulted in the lawsuit and settlement with Badri's widow. And then the conversation had shifted quickly to his own despondence at his current state— the mistakes he'd made, the miscalculations that had led him in the wrong direction since he'd left Russia. He'd told the reporter how much he missed his homeland, and how badly he wanted to return. Not to the political world, not to challenge Putin or fund a revolution or fight for democracy. Just to return home.

It wasn't simply an old man's musings after a year of tragedies, financial, personal, and legal. At some point between the end of the trial and that night at the Four Seasons, Berezovsky had taken this idea—this sudden dream—and had tried to find a way to make it a reality. To that end, he had shut himself into his office on Down Street, had sealed the double doors and set the combination, then had sat at his desk and written a letter—to Vladimir Putin.

In the letter, he had pleaded his case directly to the president. He had asked the man—the same man he had spent the past thirteen years vilifying, attacking, threatening, and blaming for countless murders—to forgive him for his actions in exile, to allow him to return to Russia. To pardon him, as a Christian, to allow him to spend his remaining years in his homeland. In the letter, he promised to stay out of politics, to be a simple mathematician. Perhaps to teach at some university, inspire a new generation to think mathematically. Even in this letter, he hadn't been able to resist offering up his services—if the president should need them—as an adviser, to help with running the country. But in the end, it was a simple request to let him come home.

He had sealed the letter in an envelope, and had passed it along to a person he knew would be able to deliver it—and had waited for a response.

As of that evening, he had heard nothing back.

Exactly, he thought, what he should have expected. A powerful man like Putin, receiving the letter of an *unimpressive* man.

Perhaps he should have ended the letter the same way he'd ended the interview with the young journalist from *Forbes*.

"I don't know what I should do," he'd told him, seeming to sink beneath his black scarf and into his dark turtleneck sweater, like a turtle into its shell. "I am sixty-seven years old. And I don't know what I should do."

I lost the meaning, he had said. The meaning of life.

Maybe he hadn't understood what he had meant. Maybe the only people who could truly understand were those who had been there, throughout it all. The players, big and small.

Alone in the bar of crimson and black, he closed his eyes and concentrated on those fingers against ivory, the scales that seemed to go on forever.

CHAPTER THIRTY-EIGHT

March 23, 2013,

Ascot, Berkshire, England

SEVENTEEN MINUTES PAST THREE in the afternoon.

A carpeted hallway bisecting the second floor of a sprawling, gated mansion in one of the most exclusive suburbs of London.

A man in a dark suit took the last few steps of the hallway at a near sprint, then hit a locked bathroom door shoulder first. The wood splintered like a bomb going off, and then the man was inside, shoes skidding against the tiled floor.

Almost immediately, he saw the body. Fully dressed, splayed out across the tiles, slight of frame but already beginning to bloat. Even from across the room, the man in the suit could make out the intense bruising around the corpse's neck, as well as the ligature digging into the skin just above the mottled throat. *A dark scarf, his favorite, according to his family, which he wore almost daily, whatever the weather.* Similar material hung from a metal shower rail, directly above.

Christ. The man in the suit blinked, hard. He knew what he was supposed to think happened here; and really, he had no reason to believe that the scene in front of him wasn't as simple as it would soon appear to the veritable brigade of police officers that would descend on this lavish mansion within the next few hours. The body on the floor, the suited man's employer of many years, whom he had last seen alive just eighteen hours earlier, had over the past few weeks become visibly depressed, despondent, and withdrawn. His final interview, which he'd given the night before, had almost been a suicide note: a despondent, lurching conversation, full of self-incrimination, dripping with desperation. A broken man, appearing even older than he actually was.

And no wonder; his boss's change in fortune over the past decade, and especially over the past few months, had been immense, the stuff of epic. This ending, a bathroom door locked from the inside, an apparent suicide by hanging, followed by the inexorable pull of gravity that had brought the body to the floor, capped a tragic spiral that probably couldn't have ended any other way.

But still, standing there in the doorway, seeing his boss lying there, cold, bruised, and twisted, it was hard not to wonder: could things really have been as simple as they seemed? And if so, how the hell had it come to this? How the hell had it all come crashing down?

The corpse on the floor had gone from being one of the richest men in the world to selling off his belongings—paintings, houses, cars—to pay off bills both professional and personal. His divorce from his second wife had cost him somewhere in the order of a quarter billion dollars. The lawsuit he had just lost had cost over one hundred million more, and there was a chance he was also on the hook for his opponent's legal feels, equally immense. He had split with his longtime partner, the Georgian, and had just finished battling his dead best friend's widow in court for a piece of her inheritance. In France, the government had taken most of his assets, at the behest of the Russian government that was trying to recoup what they accused him of having looted from a variety of businesses.

And his financial problems were only part of his descent; he had gone from being one of the most powerful kingmakers in modern history to living in a sort of gilded exile. Bodyguards, armed security, bulletproof cars and boats and planes, all were a way of life for a man who had survived multiple assassination attempts—some real, some threatened, some perhaps imagined.

Yet somehow he had always recovered, clawing his way back into history again and again. Perhaps the only real surprise here, in this second-floor bathroom, was that this dead man's third act had dragged on so long.

Whatever the truth, the man in the dark suit knew that these things were well beyond his pay grade. He was simply a bodyguard, who no longer had a body to guard. Eventually, the police investigators would arrive. They would come with radiation detectors and chemical sniffers, they would dust for fingerprints and scan for any signs of foul play. And no doubt, they would find nothing that would lead them to any conclusion beyond the most simple and obvious.

Still, no matter what the police officers found, no matter what their eventual inquest into this apparent suicide concluded, the man in the dark suit was certain that his boss wasn't killed by a scarf around his throat, a fall that broke his neck, or even by way of a sip of polonium-laced tea.

Boris Berezovsky was killed months before his corpse hit the bathroom floor, felled by a judge's gavel. A judgment not simply of a civil case—even the biggest in recorded history—but of an epic story, and the unique, ambitious, sometimes delusional man at its core.

EPILOGUE

FIFTEEN HUNDRED MILES AWAY, in an empty, wood-paneled office, atop a cavernous desk, a dark red folder lay open, revealing monogrammed pages covered in a scrawl of handwriting—letters and words carefully applied, though running together in some places, mimicking their author's style of speech. Natural light spilled across the pages, mid-morning sun leaking into the room through a sliver between the thick, heavy drapes that covered one of the office's massive windows. Sunlight caught, refracted, and then reflected by the metallic coat of arms hanging high above the desk itself—a glorious double-headed eagle, talons on one side clutching a magnificent scepter, claws on the other clutching an ornate orb. Each head bore a matching crown, with a third crown even higher.

A few feet away from the desk stood an athletic man in a perfectly tailored suit, hands clasped behind his back. He didn't relish mornings; nor did he particularly like to spend time in this office, though it lay at the heart of the country he loved, and had vowed years earlier to fiercely protect. But sometimes, this office—and that enormous desk—were an unavoidable part of his job.

As for the letter in the folder—which he had indeed read, with a mixture of amusement, pity, and maybe even disgust—well, that, on the other hand, was perfectly avoidable. Whether it would end up filed away somewhere or at the bottom of a drawer in that desk, he hadn't yet decided.

But whatever the case, he had more important things to think about than a sad, desperate, old man's letter, the etchings of an Oligarch who had enjoyed a spectacular rise—and an equally dramatic fall. In the end, in this room, in this place of true power—it was nothing more than ink on paper.

He had a long day ahead of him. A hundred problems to solve. A dozen people to meet. A handful of minor fires to put out.

A nation to rule.

He crossed the distance to the desk in two purposeful steps, and closed the folder, obscuring forever the handwritten pages inside.

BIBLIOGRAPHY

Andrews, Suzanna. "The Widow and the Oligarchs." *Vanity Fair*, October 2009.

Associated Press. "Berezovsky's Billions: How the Tycoon Lost So Much." March 26, 2013.

BBC News. "In Full: Litvinenko Statement." November 24, 2006.

———. "Timeline: Litvinenko Death Case." July 27, 2007.

Campbell, Duncan, and Tom Parfitt. "Confusion Envelops Litvinenko Even As He Goes to the Grave." *The Guardian*, December 7, 2006.

Chazan, Guy. "Russian Tycoons Face Off in Court." *The Wall Street Journal*, November 7, 2011.

China People's Daily. "Russia Publishes Kursk Sailor's Death Note." November 3, 2000.

Cowell, Alan. "Russian Ex-Spy Lived in a World of Deceptions." *The New York Times*, December 3, 2006.

European CEO. "Oleg Deripaska and the Russian Aluminum Wars." January 24, 2012.

Gardham, Duncan. "Berezovsky v Abramovich Trial: How Boris Berezovsky Lost a Fortune." *The Telegraph*, August 31, 2012.

Goldfarb, Alexander, translated by Catherine A Fitzpatrick. "Berezovsky, an Admirer's View." *The Interpreter*, May 7, 2013.

Heintz, Jim. "Videotape Shows Litvinenko Feared Retribution." *The Moscow Times*, May 24, 2007.

Helmer, John. "What the Butler (Well, Roman Abramovich's Cook) Saw." *Business Insider Australia*, November 21, 2011.

Jordan, Mary, and Peter Finn. "Russian Billionaire's Bitter Feud with Putin a Plot Line in Poisoning." *The Washington Post*, December 8, 2006.

Judah, Ben. "Behind the Scenes in Putin's Court: The Private Habits of a Latter Day Dictator." *Newsweek*, July 23, 2014.

Kara-Murza, Vladimir. "Boris Berezovsky, the Man Who Made—and Tried to Unmake—Putin." *World Affairs*, March 28, 2013.

Kramer, Andrew E. "Out of Siberia, a Russian Way to Wealth." *The New York Times*, August 20, 2006.

Kramer, Andrew. "$13 Billion Sibneft Deal Fulfills Gazprom Quest." *The New York Times*, September 29, 2005.

Landau, Elizabeth. "What Polonium Does to the Body." CNN, November 29, 2012.

Laurent, Lionel. "The Mysterious Death of Georgia's Richest Man." *Forbes*, February 14, 2008.

Leake, Christopher. "Battle of the Oligarchs: The Amazing Showdown Between Roman Abramovich and His Arch Rival." *Daily Mail Online*, October 6, 2007.

Lucas, Edward. "The New Cold War. Putin's Russia and the Threat to the West." New York: Palgrave Macmillan, 2008.

Mcallister, J. F. O. "Crime: The Spy Who Knew Too Much." *Time*, December 10, 2006.

McFee, Robin, B DO, MPH, FACPM, and Jerrold B. Leikin, MD, FACEP, FAACT, FACP, FACOEM, FACMT. "Death By Polonium 210." *Response Guide for Chemical and Radiological Threats.*

Nowak, David. "Oligarchs Take Spat to the Streets of London." *The Moscow Times*, October 9, 2007.

Parfitt, Tom, and Steven Swinford. "Boris Berezovsky's Last Interview: 'There Is No Point in Life.'" *The Telegraph*, March 24, 2013.

Sixsmith, Martin. "The Litvinenko File, Politics, Polonium, and Russia's War With Itself." New York: Macmillan, 2007.

Storr, Will. "Bad Blood: How Radioactive Poison Became the Assassin's Weapon of Choice." *Medium.com*, November 26, 2013.

The Moscow Times. "Putin Warns Oligarchs with Cudgel." October 27, 2000.

The Wall Street Journal. "Roman Abramovich by Land, Air, and Sea." September 18, 2009.

Volodarsky, Boris. "Alexander Litvinenko: A Very Russian Poisoning." *The Telegraph,* December 2, 2009.

Volodarsky, Boris. "The KGB's Poison Factory, From Lenin to Litvinenko." Chicago: Frontline Books, 2009.

Wines, Michael. "'None of Us Can Get Out', Kursk Sailor Wrote." *The New York Times,* October 27, 2000.

Zhegulev, Ilya. "Russian Oligarch Boris Berezovsky's Final Interview: 'I Want To Go Home.'" *Forbes,* Russia. Taken March 22—republished March 27, 2013, by Clare O'Connor, Forbes Staff, as translated by Denis Pinsky and Dmitri Slavinsky.

ACKNOWLEDGMENTS

*O*NCE UPON A TIME *in Russia* began with a phone call from the director/producer Brett Ratner, who told me I needed to get on a plane to London to meet someone with an incredible story to tell. I could not have imagined the adventure—both wonderful and terrifying—that would begin the minute I stepped off that British Airways flight; so first and foremost, I am indebted to Brett, whose energy and genius made this book possible. Likewise, I am extremely thankful for the generosity of my unnamed sources, who were willing to open up their lives to me during the year it took to research this book. I am in awe of the events described in this narrative, and am grateful to have been able to hear much of this story firsthand.

I am immensely grateful to Leslie Meredith, my wonderful editor; Donna Loffredo, associate editor; and the entire team at Atria/ Simon & Schuster. I am also indebted to Eric Simonoff and Matthew Snyder, agents extraordinaire. Many thanks to James Packer,

John Cheng, and everyone at Ratpac for pushing me to write the best book of my career.

As always, I am indebted to my parents, and to my brothers and their families. Special mention to Trina Palance, who helps my family run smoothly. And to Tonya, Asher, Arya, and Bugsy—this is all for you.

INDEX

ABOUT THE AUTHOR

Ben Mezrich graduated magna cum laude from Harvard. Since then he has published twelve books, including the *New York Times* bestsellers *The Accidental Billionaires*, which was adapted into the Academy Award–winning film *The Social Network*, and *Bringing Down the House*, which has sold more than 1.5 million copies in twelve languages and became the basis for the Kevin Spacey hit movie *21*. He has also published the national bestsellers *Ugly Americans*, *Rigged*, and *Busting Vegas*, and *Bringing Down the Mouse*, a book for young readers. He lives in Boston.